Bonds of Mutual Trust

bonds
of mutual trust

*The Cultural Systems of
Rotating Credit Associations
among Urban Mexicans and Chicanos*

Carlos G. Vélez-Ibañez

Rutgers University Press
New Brunswick, New Jersey

Copyright © 1983 by Rutgers, The State University of New Jersey

All rights reserved

Manufactured in the United States of America

Library of Congress Cataloging in Publication Data

Vélez-Ibañez, Carlos G., 1936–
   Bonds of mutual trust.

   Bibliography: p.
   Includes index.

   1. Rotating credit associations—Mexico.   2. Rotating
credit associations—Southwest, New.   3. Mexican
Americans.   I. Title.

HG2039.M4V44   332.2   81–17909
ISBN 0–8135–0952–1   AACR2

A mis padres.
Los primeros que me enseñaron confianza.

Contents

6 *Conclusions*   139

Illustrations

Tables

Foreword

Anthropology has always been at its best when it could place seemingly ordinary features of everyday life in a new light, and deduce unforeseen implications from that examination. This is what Carlos Vélez-Ibañez has done in his study of rotating credit associations among Mexicans and Mexican-Americans. He has not only shown the prevalence of this institution among different categories of that population, but he has demonstrated how much at variance are the resulting modes of behavior and thought from prevalent stereotypes of the shiftless poor or the distrustful Mexican. Participation in the rotating credit associations requires postponement of gratification, as well as prudential forethought. It also requires, as Vélez-Ibañez shows, "trust in the trustworthiness" of fellow participants. Vélez-Ibañez's account of how people save money through joining rotating credit associations is thus also an anthropological brief against myths that justify social discrimination by falsifying the picture of the victim.

Becoming accepted as an associate in one of these credit associations, and accepting others, depend on the cultural construct of *confianza*—the willingness to engage in generalized reciprocity with others. The concept derives from Marshall Sahlins, who saw it as a form of exchange in which gifts of goods and services are offered without the requirement of an immediate or equivalent return, in the expectation that prestations will balance out in the long run. Sahlins contrasted this form of open-ended reciprocity with "balanced reciprocity," in which a gift tended is immediately requited by a counteroffering of equal value. *Confianza* extended by the participants in a rotating credit association expresses the evaluation that offerings will continue over time, without an immediate calling in of shares extended. Trusting in each other's trustworthiness thus also expresses a shared sense that the self of each participant is culturally constructed to maximize long-term commitment and mutuality.

The social actors of Vélez-Ibañez's account adapt to their economic circumstances, but they do not do so in the Darwinian sense of winning against competitors. Rather, they engage in their arrangements of mutual credit to meet biologically and culturally defined needs through the use of a cultural invention. The rotating credit association possesses this cultural referent, even while it can be used to meet the exigencies of widely varying circumstances. Vélez-Ibañez argues that *confianza* does not constitute a bundle of culturally uniform understandings, but rather is a "cultural intersect" allowing people of quite varied backgrounds and interests to communicate sufficiently to act in concert. He thus contributes to our theoretical perspectives on culture by using an action-oriented conception in place of the older views of culture as inert tradition handed down from the dead to the living. George Herbert Mead, Marcel Mauss, A. I. Hallowell, and Erving Goffman have all shown how the self is not given a priori, but is constructed socially and culturally. Vélez-Ibañez's model, however, recalls the work of an earlier social scientist, Adam Smith, who understood that the search for utilities in the market was not carried on by atomistic maximizers, but by human beings whose behavior was constrained by what he called "propriety." Seven years before *The Wealth of Nations*, Smith wrote in his *Theory of Social Sentiment* that social interaction was governed by "sympathy," the great socializing force that ensued because each social actor, motivated by an "inner spectator" to maximize praise from others, strove to make himself praiseworthy in the eyes of the "real external spectators" who interacted with him. Sympathy gave rise to propriety, and only the desire for propriety made possible interaction in the market.

In showing how people construct notions of trustworthiness in the marketplace, Vélez-Ibañez also points to a dimension of ethnicity that goes beyond current definitions of an ethnic category as a population occupying an ecological niche or acting as a political pressure group in competition with other economic or political groups. He suggests that economics and politics also involve notions of who can be relied on and the limits of such reliance. Sometimes the very strivings to build and maintain *confianza* go awry, as Vélez-Ibañez shows in the ethnodrama. At other times there may be contradictions between the quantitative demands of the money economy and the qualitative demands of kinship, friendship, or neighborliness that underwrite the credit associations. Yet the picture of Mexicans and Mexican-Americans that Carlos Vélez-Ibañez has painted is that of people active and innovative in the pursuit of their ends, comporting themselves with dignity to meet the cultural demands of *confianza*.

Eric R. Wolf

Acknowledgments

Research carried out in 1978 and 1979 for this work was made possible by grants from the Chicano Studies Research Center and the Academic Senate at UCLA. The writing of this monograph was made possible by a fellowship from the National Chicano Council on Higher Education (NCCHE). I wish to thank Dr. Arturo Madrid who was not only responsible for the generosity of the Ford Foundation during my graduate years (1971–1974), but also for the NCCHE awards. Without these, I could not have completed either my graduate degrees or the present monograph.

To the person who was my best critic when I strayed too far off the path and who had to travel personally many of the same rocky intellectual, not to mention physical, roads leading to this work, I offer my tenderest thanks. That person is Maria Teresa Vélez, my companion and wife.

A special acknowledgment is due to Camilo Garcia Parra without whose research skills this work could not have been accomplished. I sent him out to do basic research, and he returned with such rich data that his contribution has been immeasurable. My colleagues Professors Manuel Carlos, Vernon Dixon, Ted Downing, Timothy Earle, Robert Edgerton, Paul Friedrich, Walter F. Goldschmidt, Juan Gomez-Quiñones, Larissa Lomnitz, Jane Mercer, Sally F. Moore, Michael Murphy, Michael Orbach, Thomas Weaver, B. J. Williams, and Eric R. Wolf made important substantive and critical comments during different stages of manuscript development. If I heeded some and not others, the responsibility is totally mine. I thank them all humbly.

Bonds of Mutual Trust

Introduction

Bonds of Mutual Trust analyzes a cultural invention—the rotating credit association—important to Mexicans in Mexico and the southwestern United States.[1] Like most adaptive cultural inventions, from early hunting strategies to contemporary union activities, the rotating credit association represents an attempt to reduce the uncertainty of people's lives. Even great ideologies serve this purpose: they purport to explain the basic reasons for instability and propose solutions designed to promote earthly or other-worldly stability. Mexican rotating credit associations may differ in scope from an all-embracing ideology or a basic food-gathering mechanism, but they are little different in intent from such cultural inventions.

The Mexican rotating credit association (referred to here as RCA) is known variously as *tanda, cundina, rol, rifa, bolita, mutualista, quiniela, quincela, vaca, vaquita,* and *ronda.* All these terms, which are defined later, refer to associations that range structurally from informal groups in which *confianza* (mutual trust) is the basis for participation, to intermediate organized practices in which a company's accountant or bookkeeper integrates the RCA into the payroll structure, thus combining *confianza* with market relationships, to sophisticated commercial *mutualistas* in which state laws sanction the operations of corporations that manage RCAs. All three forms of organization, however, function as savings, lending, and borrowing associations in which individuals have access to relatively large amounts of money or other valued resources while simultaneously participating in the rotation of these resources.

To understand exchange relations within these associations, it is useful to turn to Polanyi's (1957) classic categories of redistribution, reciprocity, and market exchange. To see how the mechanisms operate consider the following hypothetical informal RCA, in which all three are involved. A leader organizes among friends, neighbors, relatives, or fellow workers an association in which four other persons agree to contribute a set amount of $10 a week. The order in which resources are distributed is decided by lot or by the order in which the members agreed to join. Each person receives $40 once from the RCA. Each person will have contributed to the others $40, at the rate of $10 per week. The total life of the RCA will be five weeks. One can see from this example that the leader in some measure represents the centricity that marks the redistributive mechanism. The basis of the relationships established within the RCA, however, is *confianza*, which marks the reciprocal exchange. The medium of exchange is money (it could have been a consumer good), an indication of the market exchange mechanism. In all informally organized RCAs the cultural "glue" of *confianza* is the means by which bonds of mutual trust are maintained, and this cultural glue provides people with explicit constructs by which to fix social reality.

Mexican rotating credit associations and their underlying construct of *confianza* exemplify established practices and customs, as well as cultural expectations. But as Moore (1975: 220) has stated, "Social life presents an almost endless variety of finely distinguishable situations and quite an array of grossly different ones. It contains arenas of continuous competition. It proceeds in the context of an ever-shifting set of persons, changing movements in time, altering situations, and partially improvised interactions. Established rules, customs and symbolic frameworks exist, but they operate in the presence of areas of indeterminacy, or ambiguity, of uncertainty and manipulability. Order never fully takes over, nor could it."

From the point of view of this work, all cultural inventions, whether material or symbolic, relational or personal, represent attempts to fix these gray areas of social living by making regular the activities they include. In fact, all populations repeat, ritualize, and make regular these activities to such a degree that they seem to become matters of faith rather than matters of analysis. The repetition itself, however, is also part of the attempt to make the cultural invention stable, and is independent of the utilitarian motives or consequences involved in the invention. At the same time, however, all inventions and their constituent social activities are also mutable and transitory. Without providing any great pan-human rationalization for the ephemeral quality of all human cultural inventions, suffice it to say, as has been suggested by Leach

(1967) and Murphy (1971), that these inventions are credited by those who use them with providing stability and orderliness and that the harmony of cultural inventions is a result of analytically reducing the motion of action to coherence. Mexican rotating credit associations are little different from other cultural inventions in these regards: their constituent social activities are repeated, regularized, and sometimes linked to ritual, yet they too are transitory and mutable.

In the interplay between the attempts to stabilize social existence and the dissolution of the inventions, a dynamic learning process takes place. All human beings attempt to adapt and adjust by generating learned constructs in relation to that interplay, and these reduce the uncertainty created by such flux. Sometimes, as has been mentioned, these constructs form ideological systems, but more often than not, they become part of the important implicit lifeways of populations. They function as a lingua franca for arranging social expectations and for deciphering others' behavior. They serve as "intersects" (Schwartz 1968) in social action even though little may be culturally shared by those participating in the action.

This work deals with the learned cultural constructs that emerge from the interplay between the attempts to establish fixity and the transitory nature of the attempts. The most important constructs inferred from this research are *ahorro para ahorrar* (saving to save) and *confianza en confianza* (trust in mutual trust).[2] This literal translation of *confianza en confianza* is, however, inadequate to convey the social contexts in which the construct arises. *Confianza en confianza* has a broader meaning of trusting mutual trust. Both constructs are very important and shape the expectations used by Mexicans on both sides of the Rio Bravo (the traditional boundary separating Mexico from the United States) to define much of their social reality. Both cultural constructs are part of the tool kits used to cope with present and future social interaction. They are also prisms for goals, expectations, and needs. No cultural constructs, however, guarantee the behavior associated with them, and sometimes, as the ethnodrama in Chapter 4 illustrates, too much coherence can lead to miscommunication.

The rotating credit association is one vehicle for the articulation of these cultural constructs. Its analysis will provide insights into how a single practice leads to a series of unintended adaptive consequences that allow sizable portions of the urban Mexican population to meet sociocultural and biological needs. Such adaptive consequences provide us insights into the core of the cultural beings of many Mexicans north and south of the Rio Bravo, as well as insights into the basic human struggles of existence.

This work will establish that rotating credit associations in various forms are a widespread urban institution. They cross boundaries of class, age, sex, political units, occupations, residence, and formal institutions. As an institution the rotating credit association has the sanction of a traditional construct: *confianza*. It fulfills a variety of functions and has diverse social, cultural, psychological, economic, political, and ideological consequences. It is adaptive in diverse urban conditions. Which of its many functions and consequences dominates in a particular instance depends upon the circumstances of the people involved. In fact, the same consequences are not necessarily generated nor the same functions fulfilled even for those participating in the same association.

Some idea of the range of these consequences and functions can be gathered by considering the following list of possibilities, which are all discussed in later chapters: the associations can serve as a means to accumulate large units of capital to meet extraordinary demands as these arise; interest payments on large capital outlays can be avoided; through the associations "natural systems" can be formed in various occupational contexts, and fictive friendships in various social contexts; social credits and reciprocal networks can be generated and expanded; the associations can serve as a tool in the political strategies of people in interdependent situations; they can enable people to play games of one-upmanship against their spouses or others; where various exclusionary devices are practiced, the associations can lead to an increase in the participants' status; they can serve to integrate networks of personal relationships in institutional organizations; they can serve as an important information conduit even for activities that are not part of the associations; they can serve as a tie cross-cutting hierarchical boundaries and occupational divisions; they can form interstitial connections between classes, residential contexts, and institutional sectors, as well as between nations and regions; they can be used by Mexicans and other Hispanics in the United States to reinforce ethnic identity; they can result in the diffusion across political boundaries of the cultural construct of *confianza*; they can reduce uncertainty and indeterminacy for their participants; and finally, they will probably result in the expansion of the deutero-learned constructs of *confianza en confianza* and *ahorro para ahorrar* for all participants regardless of their reasons for participation.

1 Theoretical Issues, Cultural Constructs, and the Distribution of Rotating Credit Associations

BACKGROUND

In 1971, I first became familiar with rotating credit associations in Ciudad Netzahualcoyótl Izcalli—a city of over a million persons 17 kilometers from the center of Mexico City. Known in central urban Mexico as *tandas* (turns or rotations) and sometimes *vaquitas* (small cows or calves colloquially), RCAs appear throughout urban Mexico and in many parts of urban southwestern United States. RCAs are known by a variety of names and appear in myriad class, residential, and institutional sectors. Not as well known, however, popularly or anthropologically, are the complex economic, political, and social functions such RCAs fulfill, their variable degrees of formality and commercialization, their many intended and unintended consequences, the importance of the role the cultural construct of *confianza* plays as the adhesive for reciprocal obligations within the RCAs and the tool for stabilizing relations not yet established, and the wide extent of their distribution in urban Mexico and urban southwestern United States.

The RCA consists of "a core of participants who agree to make regular contributions to a fund which is given, in whole or in part, to each contributor in rotation" (Ardener 1964: 201). The general literature on the topic focuses on the basic functions of such practices (Anderson 1966; Ardener 1964; Gamble 1944; Geertz 1962; Kerri 1976; Kurtz and Showman 1978; Lomnitz 1977); their degree of adaptability or nonadaptability (Cope and Kurtz 1980; Kurtz 1973; Kurtz and Showman 1978; Wu 1974); their incidence in various cultures and ethnic groups (Adeyeye 1981; Ardener 1964; Asiwaju 1979; Bonnett 1976; Geertz 1962; Light 1972; Miracle, Miracle, and Cohen 1980); the methods and techniques necessary for the collection of data (Ardener 1964); and their function as "middle rung" developments in developing economies (Geertz 1962; Light 1972; Lomnitz 1977; Morton 1978; Wu 1974).

The two seminal works by Geertz (1962) and Ardener (1964) explain the emergence of rotating credit associations from opposite viewpoints. Geertz emphasizes a developmental construct. He suggests that such practices generally emerge during the "shift from a traditionalistic agrarian society to an increasingly fluid commercial one" after the interpretation of market and trade relations (260–261). One important consequence of such a development is that peasants engaged in such practices learn "rational" economic measures (261). Ardener, on the other hand, points out that the emergence of such associations is important in some societies that have made the transition to trading economies but not in others (221). In addition, she suggests that in some urban associations in South Africa, "nonrational" feasting and social prestige are stressed rather than strictly economic relations and processes. Thus, she argues that the Parsonian notions that Geertz uses to define learning shifts are likely to lead nowhere analytically (223).

The data in this work illustrate that in both the United States and Mexico, ritual activity and gift giving are important parts of the associations, and that the associations are not simply tied to the members' economic motives. In fact, an important consideration in the analysis of the various forms of the associations found in this research is that without a willingness to engage in generalized reciprocal relations based on mutual trust, the associations could not function. As Sauliniers (1976) has shown in his analysis of urban reciprocal prestation systems in Zaire, education and long-term urban residence, which are usually indicators of modernization, contribute to the reinforcement, not the decline, of traditional prestation systems. Therefore, to consider the various forms of the rotating credit associations as institutions in which "traditional" populations learn "modern" attitudes of an economic sort does not seem to be a fruitful strategy. Cognitive learning does indeed occur, but in a different form from that postulated by Geertz.

Another element should be considered in sorting out questions of a cross-cultural sort. Geertz (1962: 260) has admitted that in all cases with which he was familiar, such associations probably spread by diffusion. Yet he states that diffusion analysis does not contribute to our understanding of the social functioning of the associations themselves. From the point of view postulated here, whether practices emerge from a set of conditions or are diffused does not prevent the analysis of their intended and unintended social functions. Diffusion analysis may not provide causal explanations for the emergence of the rotating credit associations cross-culturally, yet it can provide clues about what structural and cultural conditions must occur in their point of origin for such practices to spread.

The associations in this analysis are all urban forms and emerge within a variety of class contexts. There are many structural and historical reasons for their emergence, including, for example, the necessity of rotating scarce resources in marginal and working-class sectors or extending strained resources in middle-class contexts. Yet, such forms are diffused by migrating populations from urban areas in Mexico to other urban areas in Mexico and to urban areas in the United States. It is more than likely that for such migrating urban populations, the structural and cultural conditions responsible for the emergence of the associations are not appreciably different in the new settings from what they were in their points of origin. In fact, for Mexicans migrating to the United States an added structural variable—ethnic discrimination—may contribute to the emergence of such reciprocal practices. Wu (1974) has suggested a similar proposition for Chinese in New Guinea.

Clearly the origin, function, and operation of such associations in Africa, Asia, the West Indies, the Americas, and Europe cannot be explained by reference to theories of social transformation or diffusion alone. Explanations must include not just theories of a causal sort, as Geertz has tried to do, but also diffusion analysis, which traces these associations to their point of origin to discover the structural or cultural conditions from which they emerged. Even within the same region both explanations may be necessary. In the United States three versions of the rotating credit association coexist, which were brought to Los Angeles, California, from China, Japan, and Mexico. Yet their points of origin were at entirely different stages of industrialization and modernization when these practices were carried by migrating populations. China and Japan were both agricultural societies, and the migrating populations were made up of peasants. The Mexican versions, on the other hand, were carried to the United States by twentieth-century urban migrants to border cities and states. Combining causal explanations and diffusion analysis is especially efficacious if the latter can be related to proven cross-cultural theories. Learning theory, for example, might be included as a construct within diffusion analysis and might provide insights contributing to the discovery of theoretically sound principles.

Among the important discoveries made in this research is that Mexicans have generated a variety of different forms of such practices never before reported in the Mexican literature. These include informally organized rotating credit associations, intermediate types, and formally organized commercialized RCAs administered by private and civil corporations. Central issues to be addressed are the crucial nature of the reciprocal exchange relation as a central mode of exchange in informal RCAs, which is an important key to understanding their widespread distribution; the recognition of the important adaptive functions and resultant consequences of RCAs in different urban contexts; and the uncertain conditions existing in the contexts in which RCAs appear. These conditions emerge in different forms which vary according to the structure of the contexts in which they appear. The last issue discussed is that the interplay between such indeterminate conditions and attempts at regularizing and fixing social reality will result in adaptively learned cultural constructs of *confianza en confianza* and *ahorro para ahorrar*.

METHODS AND TECHNIQUES

This study results from data collected in the field between 1971 and 1974, during the summer of 1978, throughout 1979, and during part of 1980. The data, which cover 90 informal, intermediate, and formal rotating credit associations, representing approximately 4,000 persons, were gathered from more than 60 informants in 17 cities and 2 countries.[1]

Two types of techniques were used for the field studies: personal contacts available from previous fieldwork, through friends, and from established consanguineous, affinal, and professional relationships, provided the initial introduction to the RCAs. We thus gained entry into diverse social sectors in Mexico and southwestern United States. Each contact point led to numerous RCAs which in turn led to many other RCAs. As a result representative examples of the RCA and a broad spectrum of social sectors of which they were a part were sampled. Second, "judgment" (Honigmann 1970: 268–269) and "chance" sampling were used. People encountered in taxis, on commensal and ritual occasions, in entertainment and recreational centers, in hotels and restaurants, on queues in banks, at food centers and bus stops, in commercial institutions and public places, as well as at professional meetings and informal gatherings, were all tapped. For example, a chance encounter with the psychiatrist of a neighborhood friend provided access to RCAs. This work derives from an extensive range of universes, which probably represents almost all the social sectors in which RCAs operate. As a result general statements may be made concerning the main theoretical issues raised that cross geographical, social, and economic boundaries.

Data were systematically collected through questionnaires when appropriate. When the occasion was unsuitable, as in bars, taxis, queues, or with brief acquaintances, the organization of the questionnaire was followed. (To whip out a questionnaire in a working-class bar amid the laments of Mexican music would have been inappropriate.) Curiously, however, people did not generally object to the use of a tape recorder, regardless of context.

CONFIANZA

One informant referred to rotating credit associations as "*una unión de confianza*" (a bond of mutual trust), which is highly significant because, despite the occurrence of specific economic transactions, the basis of the associations is a social exchange.[2] This is emphasized in the exchange relationship, and it is a widely understood and valued requirement for the smooth operation of many RCAs among Mexicans north and south of the Rio Bravo. The term *confianza* (see Lomnitz's excellent discussions, 1971, 1977) signifies a cultural construct in which are contained numerous factors, among them the willingness of persons to stand in a reciprocal relationship with one another. Like any other human construct, it expands in use and evolves along with the social networks in which it occurs, so that *confianza* within some social sectors will be variable in function. Yet this willingness to initiate

an exchange of reciprocity is crucial to understanding the poten-
tialities of the rotating credit associations and their widespread
geographical distribution.

The cultural construct of *confianza* is a subjective, descriptive
cultural understanding analogous to Polanyi's (1957) analytical
construct of the reciprocal exchange mode and Sahlins's (1969)
construct of "generalized reciprocity." Among Mexicans in Mexico
and in the United States, *confianza* designates generosity and intimacy as well as a personal investment in others; it also indicates
a willingness to establish such generosity and intimacy. It is a general construct which is projected and sought and even includes
those with whom no actual intimacy has been established. This
last assertion contradicts Lomnitz, but in this work *confianza* indicates more than relationships in which favors, confidences, or
assistance have actually been exchanged. Lomnitz has described
confianza's key elements in the following way:

> A person feels *confianza* in another when he trusts the other to have
> the ability, the desire, and the good disposition to initiate a personal
> relationship of *reciprocity exchange*, or when his own familiarity with
> the other would encourage him to make the first approach himself.
> Such an initial move usually consists of requesting a favor or in offer-
> ing to perform a favor without risking a misinterpretation of this
> gesture. Another form of expressing *confianza* is the act of volun-
> teering an item of personal information of an intimate character, thus
> implying faith in the discretion and friendly disposition of the other
> person (1977: 196–197; emphasis added).

Lomnitz uses Sahlins's definitional contrasts between "generalized reciprocity" and "balanced reciprocity" to flesh out the degree
and intensity of *confianza*. Generalized reciprocity is an exchange
in which people give each other material items, favors, or labor
without expecting anything in return at that time or in the immediate future. Balanced reciprocity is an exchange in which the
items, favors, or labor have a precise worth and the reciprocated
exchange is equivalent to the item received and is made without
delay (Sahlins 1969: 147–148). The fact that the money or items
exchanged and the duration of the rotating credit associations are
explicitly stated would place the operations of the associations
within the balanced reciprocity relation. However, while this definition may provide a valid analytical boundary between general-

ized and balanced reciprocity, the cultural construct of *confianza* which allows the rotating credit association to emerge and function is actually generalized mutual trust. Negotiations, transformations, compacts, conviviality, and specific needs ultimately determine the actual nature of *confianza* in specific contexts, but the construct of *confianza* as a core expectation begins as a generalized reciprocal construct. Rotating credit associations may be engaged in balanced reciprocal exchanges, but such exchanges could not occur unless more general expectations of mutual trust (*confianza*) of a diffuse sort were present. These general reciprocal expectations have a variety of culturally constituted safeguards, as later analysis will demonstrate.

Confianza, then, is the psychocultural construct organizing expectations for intended relationships, and it patterns social and political interpersonal and exchange networks among Mexicans in the United States and Mexico. It is basic to such Mexican social categories and types of relationships as *compadrazgo* (cogodparenthood), *amistad* or *cuatismo* (friendship or palship), *padrino político* (political godfather; Carlos and Anderson 1981), *asesor* or *coyote* (consultant or broker), or *cacique* (political figure and broker; Carlos and Anderson 1981; Lomnitz 1977). Although varying in organizational influence, the *confianza* construct does provide a formula of reciprocity for each of these social categories and their relationships. As these unfold in social processes and events, these relationships—equal and unequal—express the reciprocal exchange mode in varying degrees. Whether used in exchanges involving power or affection, the *confianza* construct patterns the initial willingness to reciprocate not only between dyads but in contacts that go far beyond known and established relationships.

As a construct it organizes expectations of relationships within broad networks of interpersonal links in which intimacies, favors, goods, services, emotion, power, or information are exchanged. Whether such exchanges are expressed in political domains between patrons and clients or in intimate relationships between friends, *confianza* is the core principle underlying their development and stability, and at times, part of the agent responsible for their dissolution. Finally, *confianza* selects for an organized means of forming predictable expectations about relationships. How such relationships are actually transformed and negotiated is a processual and structural matter.

Open, Processual, and Closed Confianza

Cultural expectations are not usually maintained unless they are given life in social relationships. On the one hand, no social relationship is ever tidy or totally coherent. The processual reality for most social relationships is that they are initially "open" in the sense that little has been settled by the actors that would define the exchanges as being of one sort or another. Even when such definitions occur, however, other relationships from other contexts affect those being established between any two actors. On the other hand, some relationships, such as kinship relations, are "given"; in these definitions are marked, expectations defined, and exchanges relatively predictable. Yet even "closed" relations are also affected by a host of other relationships from other contexts.

Confianza as a cultural construct is an expectation about relationships. It is given its open or closed character by the sorts of exchanges in which any two actors engage, the time such exchanges have been in operation, the social and economic context in which such relations are articulated, and very importantly, the effect *other* relationships have on those being established, those already established, or those in the process of dissolution. No matter how closed *confianza* relationships may appear, they are still affected by a host of other relationships.

The point to be stressed here is that while *confianza* is a psychocultural expectation, it is given life by the state of existing social relationships, the nature of the relationships being transacted, and the stability or instability of any set of relationships for a set of actors who have *confianza*. No such relationships, however, are ever fixed in a totally predetermined or certain pattern. While *confianza* is a construct for organizing predictable expectations about relationships, the construct is sufficiently flexible and inclusive to allow the reality of social living to change its boundaries for any actor or set of actors.

When relationships are first initiated, they will be marked by "open *confianza*," in which so much is indeterminate and uncertain that actors give each other a wide berth for mistakes and faux pas. For example, recent urban migrants will seek out others with whom to establish *confianza*, and many different contexts and types of exchanges will be tried out and experimented with. Those contexts and exchanges that prove to be most rewarding will be retained as proper for the type of *confianza* established between any two actors. Once established, however, that *confianza* is not necessarily embedded perpetually, for the reasons given. Nevertheless, as *confianza* relationships articulated between friends, for example, become expected and the nature of the exchanges relatively defined, these *confianza* relationships are introduced into already established closed *confianza* relationships, such as those between kin, or into other open *confianza* relationships. Thus any two friends for whom *confianza* has been established will in turn establish that friendship with other friends and kinfolk. During the process of contacting other networks of relationships, *confianza* becomes a "processual *confianza*" in that others are commenting upon and evaluating the persons engaged in the friendship. It is during the period of processual *confianza* that the politics of exchange will occur, that claims of worthiness or unworthiness are made, and that friendships become articulated within previously established relatively close *confianza* relationships.

For a time such relationships will be part of the actors' relatively closed networks of relationships, and *confianza* between those two actors will be closed to others, at least at the conscious level of exchange. However, closure is illusionary since even the most closed relationships are open to the unintended consequences of the actions of others, to changing economic and social conditions, and to the failure of expectations to be met.

There is no necessary continuum between open, processual, and closed *confianza*. At any stage of development, open *confianza* can be disrupted by the unintended consequences mentioned. Processual *confianza* can be interrupted by the judgments of those in closed *confianza*, or other open *confianza* relationships can seem more rewarding. Closed *confianza* relationships can be disrupted by an immigration raid among undocumented immigrants in the United States, or as the case discussed in Chapter 4 illustrates, the density of *confianza* may very well lead to the rupture of *confianza* relations since in such relationships sources of conflicts are not aired.

Confianza, then, is a dynamic psychocultural construct in that its boundaries change with changing conditions. It is therefore ultimately very selective for the populations who share it. For urban Mexicans, in the United States or Mexico, *confianza* is an especially positively selective construct given the pressures of mobility, economic conditions, and ethnic relations. *Confianza* fixes and establishes expectations above relationships in most uncertain and indeterminate contexts in a predictable manner, but it is a sufficiently flexible construct to change as contexts become more certain or social relations more determinate.

Conditions for Confianza *and Reciprocity*

Lomnitz has suggested that *confianza* is especially prevalent among large urban populations such as the marginally poor, in which institutionalized means are inadequate for establishing security (1977: 198). However, an important discovery in our research was that *confianza* and the reciprocal exchange mode transcend the class sectors with which Lomnitz was concerned. Lomnitz and Pérez (1974) have analyzed reciprocal exchange used by Mexican upper-class sectors to preserve or increase corporate interests, and Carlos (1973) and Carlos and Anderson (1981) have analyzed the dynamic penetration of reciprocal interpersonal relationships and networks into institutional domains. No previous work has used a single mechanism, as the rotating credit association is used here, to illustrate the existence of reciprocity in which *confianza* is the cement for social relations in a variety of class, residential, and institutional sectors.

The issue here is that there are underlying conditions that give rise to such practices as RCAs, their reciprocal mechanisms, and the cultural construct of *confianza*. For Lomnitz (1977: 191) "a condition of balanced scarcity [is] assumed to persist indefinitely for both partners." She has also stated that such conditions are present when persons "live beyond their means," as in middle-class sectors. I would argue that these are sufficient but not necessary conditions for the rise of the reciprocal mode and such practices as the RCA. The necessary and sufficient conditions are those in which uncertainty of context, indeterminacy of relationships, scarcity of resources, or ambiguity of statuses occur. Uncertain contexts are those in which a lack of information makes it impossible to form coherent expectations (Orbach 1979). Indeterminacy of relationships refers to the manipulative or negotiable aspects of all relationships. Most contexts have some degree of uncertainty, and all relationships have room for negotiation and manipulation.

GEOGRAPHICAL DISTRIBUTION

Lewis (1959: 68, 148; 1961: 453; 1968: 214) first reported the Mexican version of the RCA, *tanda* (turn), among the *vecindades* (neighborhoods) of Mexico City, but unfortunately did little analysis of the practice or its distribution. From fieldwork data collected during 1968–1969, Kurtz (1973) reported the *cundina* (from the verb *cundir* to spread) and *rol* (roll?), both versions of the RCA among Mexicans in San Ysidro, California, and Tijuana, Baja California. As mentioned, I first encountered the *tanda* quite accidentally in a casual conversation in Ciudad Netzahualcoyótl Izcalli. Interestingly Lomnitz had been gathering data on the *tanda* at roughly the same time in Cerrada del Condor in Mexico City, which she reported later in her outstanding work, *Networks and Marginality* (1977).

My first glimpses of the RCAs gave no hint of their widespread geographical distribution, and even when I consulted various sources in the National Anthropology Library and the National Library in Mexico City, I found nothing to indicate their widespread distribution. In 1978, Kurtz and Showman (66) reported that the *tanda* was common in the city of Puebla and the municipalities of San Felipe Hueyotlipan and San Jéronimo Caleras which are adjacent suburbs of Puebla. The participants in the *tandas* came from a wide spectrum of social backgrounds: blue- and white-collar workers including factory workers, bank employees, seamstresses, store clerks, housewives, food vendors, and so on.

My data show that RCAs are distributed extensively throughout urban Mexico and parts of the urban U.S. Southwest; they have also been reported in Guatemala and Peru.[3] Guatemalan workers living on the West Coast of the United States told me about a Guatemalan version known as a *cuchuval* (from the Quichee *cuchu* meaning congregation or reunion and *val*, to raise; see de Bourbourg 1862: 174, 229). These informants indicated that in Tecunuman (in the department of San Marcos), low-paid workers in factories and large commercial concerns organized such associations. They said also that they participated in Mexican RCAs in Los Angeles, where they were known as *cundinas* (from the verb *cundir*, to spread). This was not the term used in Guatemala and was specific to the Mexicans with whom they associated at work, in the neighborhood, and in recreational activities. It is significant that these Guatemalan workers participated with Mexican workers in rotating credit associations and that both groups were illegal immigrants. Both groups thus suffered from a high degree of uncertainty.

I discovered how consistently the Mexican RCA crops up among urban Mexicans serendipitously in the course of another investigation. I was testing the hypothesis that where Chinese contract workers established residence in Mexico after 1899, a Chinese version of the RCA, termed *hui*[4] would also appear. I hypothesized that in those areas from which the Chinese were not expelled,[5] the *hui* would take root as it had in other parts of the world like New Guinea, Britain, and the United States.[6]

According to Ching Chieh Chang (1956: 56–59), Chinese labor had eventually settled in the major cities of the extreme southern areas of Mexico, such as Tapachula, Chiapas, and Mérida, Yucatán; and in the North in Tampico, Tamaulipas; Monterrey, Nuevo León; Mexicali, Baja California; and Chihuahua, Chihuahua. I did research in all these cities and states except Tampico and found a number of rotating credit associations in each city. Only one definite relationship could be established with the Chinese *hui*, but it was insufficient to verify the original hypothesis.

Research also uncovered RCAs in Guanajuato, Guanajuato; Guadalajara, Jalisco; Papantla, Jalapa, and Poza Rica, Veracruz; Ciudad Júarez, Chihuahua; Ensenada, Baja California; Saltillo, Coahvilla; Culiacán, Mazatlán, and Concordia, Sinaloa. Rotating credit associations were also discovered in El Paso, Texas; Chula Vista, National City, San Diego, Hollywood, Beverly Hills, San Pedro, Wilmington, West Los Angeles, East Los Angeles, and much of metropolitan Los Angeles, California. One informant also reported the existence of RCAs in Chicago.

The published literature and personal research in Ciudad Netzahualcoyótl Izcalli and the Federal District of Mexico turned up other rotating credit associations. One informant who had been a traveling salesman indicated that such practices were also common in San Cristobal de las Casas and Tuxtla Gutiérrez, Chiapas; Oaxaca, Oaxaca; Puebla, Puebla; and Tonalá, Jalisco. The associations Kurtz (1973) identified in Tijuana and San Ysidro were verified in my research.

From the primary data collected in my research and the references of other investigators, RCAs can be definitely accounted for in 35 urban or suburban municipalities in the Republic of Mexico and the United States. Reports by informants reliably identify 5 other urban or suburban municipalities as having such practices. Thus of 40 sites investigated, 28 Mexican urban or suburban municipalities and 13 United States communities can be reliably identified as having such practices. The map pinpoints the occurrence of such practices.

Thirteen of the 26 Mexican states can be reliably said to have such associations, as do Mexico City and the Federal District. North of the Rio Bravo, the practice seems quite well established in California and Texas. The literature has not reported such practices occurring in Arizona, New Mexico, or Colorado, nor have personal inquiries proved fruitful.[7] California has probably the most extensive distribution of RCAs in the United States because of the heavy migration of Mexicans into that area. The greatest concentration is probably to be found in the San Diego area, which includes the city of San Diego itself, Chula Vista, National City, and San Ysidro. In the Los Angeles area, the greatest concentration seems to be in San Pedro, Wilmington, East Highlands, East Los Angeles, and portions of central Los Angeles. In addition, I would predict that Chicago, Detroit, urban centers in Indiana, and other midwestern regions that attract large numbers of Mexican workers will also have such associations.

The geographical distribution, then, illustrates that RCAs are found frequently in either highly urbanized sectors or suburban areas adjacent to large urban centers in Mexico and the United States. It is highly likely that such associations are not present in rural sectors of either Mexico or the United States. Such associations may very well be present, however, in agricultural sectors with industrially based productive modes and in the adjacent small towns (see Goldschmidt 1976). The municipalities of San Felipe Hueyotlipan and San Jerónimo Caleras have populations of only 7,000 persons each, yet are largely composed of wage laborers

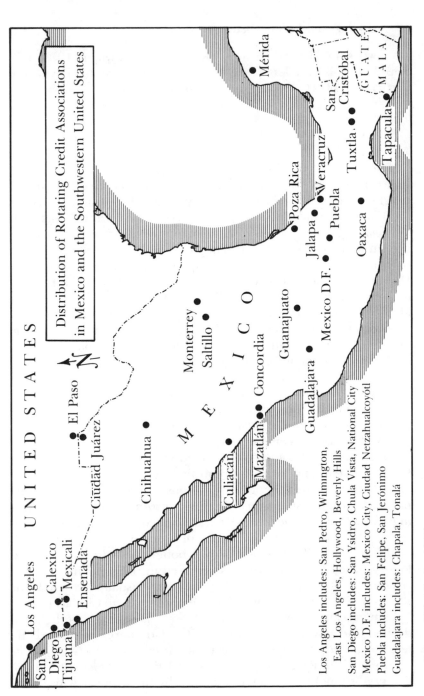

UNITED STATES

Distribution of Rotating Credit Associations
in Mexico and the Southwestern United States

Los Angeles
San
Diego
Tijuana
Calexico
Mexicali
Ensenada

El Paso
Ciudad Juárez

Chihuahua

M E X I C O

Mazatlán
Concordia

Culiacán

Monterrey
Saltillo

Guanajuato

Guadalajara

Mexico D.F.

Jalapa
Puebla

Oaxaca

Poza Rica
Veracruz

Tuxtla

San
Cristóbal

Tapacula

Mérida

G U A T E
M A L A

Los Angeles includes: San Pedro, Wilmington,
  East Los Angeles, Hollywood, Beverly Hills
San Diego includes: San Ysidro, Chula Vista, National City
Mexico D.F. includes: Mexico City, Ciudad Netzahualcoyotl
Puebla includes: San Felipe, San Jerónimo
Guadalajara includes: Chapala, Tonalá

Source: Vélez-Ibáñez 1982b.

who work in factories nearby (Kurtz and Showman 1978: 66). Population size is a less reliable indicator of the probability of the occurrence of RCAs than the productive mode.

NOMENCLATURE

The names of the associations vary by geographical area. Sometimes the names are used interchangeably to denote other similar practices of saving or cooperative pooling. For example, RCAs are known as *tandas* (turns) in Monterrey, and local variants such as *ronda*, *quiniela*, or *quincela*, are interchanged with *tandas* in the same area. A *ronda* is usually a round of a game or drinks, or contributions, while a *quiniela* is more strictly a betting pool. *Quincela* is a derivative of the word *quincena* (fortnight). Thus *quincela* refers to the distribution of money in the associations after each semimonthly payday. However, some informants in Monterrey consistently used the term *quiniela* for *tanda* while only one distinguished *quiniela* as a betting pool from the RCA or *tanda*. Another informant stated that *quiniela* and *ronda* were used interchangeably with *tanda*, but during the course of the interview, she consistently used the term *tanda*.

Because of the problem of variation of usage, it is necessary to pinpoint the location of terms as well as variant uses. This discussion will provide a general guide for other researchers, and their findings may verify, add to, or provide alternative interpretations for the sources and locations identified here.

In Ciudad Juárez the local variations of nomenclature became particularly interesting since there were so many varieties of savings and lottery practices. *Quiniela* seemed to be the preferred term. There were various versions of lotteries such as the *vaquita* (small cow or calf) in which people bought a share of a national lottery ticket. Some informants referred to the standard *tanda* as *vaquita* or *vaca* (cow), but the *vaca* was usually reserved for RCAs in El Paso, Texas, which is the border city to Ciudad Juárez.

Female employees in the *maquiladoras* (labor-intensive light industry) and government offices in Ciudad Juárez preferred the term *quiniela*. At times, informants used the phrase *cajas de ahorros* for the RCAs, but most agreed that the *cajas* were more like credit unions formally established by the firm for which they worked or informally by the workers themselves. In the *cajas*, unlike the RCA, there was no set amount that had to be contributed. On the other hand, in some offices, women and only women combined *quinielas* (RCAs) with the practice of *regalos* (gift giving, especially on saints' days and birthdays), and with monthly commensal activities in which cakes and pies were also exchanged. All three practices, however, operated unrecognized within these institutions.

One informant who had extensive knowledge of savings and lottery practices in Ciudad Juárez distinguished between *quinielas, cajas de ahorros,* and *tandas.* He stated that the *quiniela* was a type of lottery in which 100 or so people participated in a drawing in which there was only one winner, while the *caja de ahorros* was an informally organized credit union. He had often seen this operating among bartenders and waitresses. *Tandas* were restricted to those who earned higher wages, and the practices were those of the standard informally organized RCA. In contrast, however, 5 persons interviewed in an industrial park area were not familiar with the term *tanda* but knew the practice as *quiniela.* A taxi driver said that the *quiniela* was the one used in his chauffeurs' association. Of those interviewed, all but one agreed that the term *quiniela* was preferred. Two of these 5 people had been organizers of RCAs and were most reliable informants.

The data on RCAs in Chihuahua are limited to informants. These informants, however, had lived in the city for many years, knew it extremely well, and had organized RCAs not only in residential areas but in a variety of places of employment and recreation. They stated that in Chihuahua the preferred term was *tanda* and that other terms were inappropriate since *quiniela* referred to a lottery and *cajas de ahorros* to types of credit unions. Independently, informants agreed that *tandas* were quite widespread in Chihuahua and that many people were familiar with them, even though not all participated. It seems fair to state that the term *tanda* is the standard one for RCAs in Chihuahua.

Informants independently agreed that the *tanda* had been diffused from the south of Mexico and was not limited to or original in northern Mexico. This suggests that migrants from the South could have introduced the practice to northern Mexico, which would be in keeping with the patterns of migration to the area (Weaver and Downing 1977).

In Sinaloa, however, one of Mexico's northwestern states, informants used the term *cundina*. Informants in Culiacán and Mazatlán stated that the term had been used by the previous generation so that the practice must have been operating for at least 60 years at the time our data were gathered in 1979. *Cundinas* also occur in Concordia, Sinaloa, a small rural town between the cities of Culiacán and Mazatlán.

In central Mexico, which includes the Federal District, Mexico City, and Ciudad Netzahualcoyótl, the popular term is *tanda*. Our informants, including a government economist, a labor organizer, a sociology graduate student, low-level government employees, museum employees, upper-class housewives, retired upper-middle-class networks, hotel employees, taxi drivers, and people in numerous queues in banks, subways, and movie houses all verified the preference for the term *tanda*. *Vaca* or *vaquita* was, however, used synonymously by some informants. Some *tandas* in this area were known specifically by their purpose. In *tandas de Volkswagen*, for example, a Volkswagen Beetle is distributed as the share, and *tandas de Casa* (home RCAs) as well as *tandas de Datsun* were also mentioned.

In the Leucunberry prison, Mexico's most infamous jail for political prisoners, a *vaca* or *vaquita* was a cooperative savings group organized to buy larger amounts of marijuana (cannabis of whatever species) within the prison for a discount. Unlike the standard *tanda*, the *vaca* or *vaquita* was not necessarily made up of individual equal shares although this was the preferred form. If equal shares were not possible, then the amount of marijuana doled out was equal to the amount contributed. Thus, besides Volkswagen and Datsun *tandas*, *Cannabis mexicana vacas* seem to have been the most specialized.

In Guadalajara, *tanda* was preferred. Informants who had lived in the city and had participated as organizers and participants for over 30 years all indicated that *tanda* was the only term used, but the term *rifa* (raffle) was also used by an ex-organizer to describe rotating credit associations. One informant, a traveling saleswoman who traveled extensively between Guadalajara and Chihuahua, verified that *quiniela* was the term used in Ciudad Juárez and *tanda* in Chihuahua. A sample of nine other people including a university student, a bank clerk, a proletarian housewife, a secretary, an anthropologist, a ceramicist, a hotel employee, a petty merchant, a businessman, and a high school student all indicated that *tanda* was the preferred term. Nearby in Tonalá and Chapala, *tanda* was again the term used.

Further south, in the state of Veracruz, the informants in the cities of Poza Rica, Papantla, and Jalapa preferred the term *tanda* also, although specialized uses required more specific nomenclature. Thus a *tanda de cuates* (an RCA of pals) is a very small one for no more than five persons whose specific goal is to purchase alcoholic beverages, from which results as an unintended consequence prestige for the person who can consume the most alcohol without becoming intoxicated.

The term *bolita* (little ball) was used occasionally by informants, generally to describe RCAs in which 40 or more participated. The term came from the numbered balls used in randomly selecting the order of distribution of the share fund to the members. Regardless of the term used, informants who had participated and organized *tandas* for 15 years all agreed that the term *tanda* was used in Veracruz and that it was strictly an urban practice and not known to *gente de rancho* (persons from rural areas).

Among the most elaborate and commercialized RCAs are those found in Mérida. In Mérida, the term *mutualista* is used to describe both informal and formal commercial associations. It is also used to describe funerary associations, which are not rotating credit associations. Both informally and formally organized RCAs are prevalent in Mérida.

In Tapachula, the term *tanda* is most frequently used although one informant used *quiniela* interchangeably, as well as *rol* and *poya* (share or amount due). This should be considered exceptional. In Tapachula, informants of Chinese descent admitted to being familiar with the Chinese *hui*. Most stated that their forebears had participated in China but did not recall such associations in the Chinese colony in Tapachula. Yet the reticence of the informants does lead one to suspect that the local associations of *paisanos*, as the Chinese refer to themselves in Mexico, do in fact have *hui* in operation. Others of Chinese descent indicated very strongly that the Chinese *hui* had not been introduced into Mexico and that all Chinese were assimilated into Mexican life. Yet the local Chinese benevolent association met to consider cooperation with this research. The strength of their denial and the fact that organizations based on Chinese descent exist suggest that a great deal of fear of Mexican chauvinism may still be felt and for very good historical reasons (see note 5, this chapter).

Although material collected in this research substantiated Kurtz's findings of the RCA in the San Diego-Tijuana area, it showed transnational characteristics not explored by Kurtz. In addition, *cundinas* were found in Ensenada and Mexicali, B.C. Our informants, however, did not use the word *rol*, as Kurtz indicated, but instead used only *cundina*. Informants did refer to newspaper articles in which the term *tanda* was used. These findings do not negate Kurtz's original discovery; our informants simply were not familiar with the term *rol*.

The term *cundina* is widespread in the San Diego area, and the data in part were generated from the city of Chula Vista which is between San Diego and San Ysidro-Tijuana. In addition there are commuter *cundinas* that cross the borders between Tijuana and Chula Vista. Our informants in Chula Vista had participated in such practices for over 20 years in both the United States and Mexico. All agreed that the preferred term was *cundina*, and some were familiar with the word *tanda*. They nevertheless made careful distinctions between *cundinas* and *mutualistas*. The latter were strictly funerary associations and not rotating credit associations.

In San Pedro, Wilmington, and Hollywood, which are incorporated into Los Angeles City, *cundina* was the preferred term. This wa also the case in Beverly Hills, central city Los Angeles, and West Los Angeles. Nevertheless, there were informants who were familiar with the term *tanda* as the proper nomenclature, and it is more than likely that these people had come from the central or southern areas of Mexico. (Two informants stated that in their state of Guanajuato in central Mexico *tanda* was the normal usage while *cundina* was used exclusively in downtown Los Angeles.) On the other hand, one informant who had learned the practice in the United States simply called it *ahorro* (saving).

This *ahorro*, however, should not be confused with the savings cooperatives formed by Chicano steelworkers during World War II. Such noninstitutionalized savings cooperatives were modeled after the Liga Obrera Mexicana (see note 7, this chapter), but the steelworker cooperatives dissolved because so many participants were drafted into the army.

Table 1.1 summarizes the nomenclature discovered in this research and that reported previously by others. The table includes

Table 1.1. Nomenclature by Area

Principal Term	Area	City	Variants
Tanda: *muerta–viva* *fuerte–pequeña*	northern Mexico	Monterrey, Nuevo León	*ronda, quiniela,* *quincela, rol*
Tanda	northern Mexico	Saltillo, Coahuilla	none known
Cundina: *fuerte–pequeña*	northern Mexico	Mexicali, Tijuana, and Ensenada, Baja California	*rol, tanda*[1]
Quiniela	northern Mexico	Ciudad Juárez, Chihuahua	*caja de ahorros*
Tanda: *fuerte–pequeña*	northern Mexico	Chihuahua, Chihuahua	none known
Cundina	northern Mexico	Concordia, Mazatlán, and Culiacán, Sinaloa	none known
Tanda: *muerta–viva* *fuerte–pequeña*	central Mexico	Mexico City,[2] Federal District, Ciudad Netzahual- coyótl, state of Mexico	*vaca, vaquita*
Tanda	central Mexico	Guanajuato, Guanajuato	none known
Tanda	central Mexico	Puebla,[3] San Felipe, and San Jerónimo, Puebla	none known
Tanda	south-central Mexico	Guadalajara, Chapala, and Tonalá Jalisco	*rifa*
Mutualista: informal–formal	southern Mexico (Gulf side)	Mérida, Yucatán	*caja de ahorros*
Tanda: *muerta–viva*	southern Mexico (Gulf side)	Poza Rica, Papantla, and Jalapa, Veracruz	*bolita*
Tanda	southern Mexico (Guatemala side)	Tapachula, San Cristóbal de la Casas, and Tuxtla Gutiérrez, Chiapas	none known
Tanda	southern Mexico (Guatemala side)	Oaxaca, Oaxaca	none known
Vaca	southwestern United States	El Paso, Texas	*vaquita*

Table 1.1. Nomenclature by Area

Principal Term	Area	City	Variants
Cundina	southwestern United States	San Diego, San Ysidro,[1] Chula Vista, and National City, California	*rol, tanda*
Cundina	Mexico-U.S. border region	Tijuana-San Diego area	*tanda*
Cundina	southwestern United States	Los Angeles,[5] San Pedro, Wilmington, Hollywood, and Beverly Hills, California	*tanda, ahorro*
Cundina	southwestern United States	unincorporated East Los Angeles	*tanda*
Cuchuval	northern Guatemala	Tecúnuman, San Marcos	none known
Pandero	Peru	Lima,[6] Huancayo	junta

1. Reported by Kurtz (1973) and, except for the term *rol*, verified by this research.

2. Reported by Lewis (1959, 1961, 1968) and Lomnitz (1977) and verified by this research.

3. Reported by Kurtz and Showman (1978) and Cope and Kurtz (1980).

4. Reported by Kurtz (1973) and verified by this research, with the added discovery of transnational commuter associations.

5. Includes West Los Angeles.

6. See note 3, Chapter 1 for details.

four terms not discussed here: *muerta-viva* (dead-alive) and *fuerte-pequeña* (strong-weak). The former pair, as will be discussed shortly, refers to commercial as opposed to noncommercial informal RCAs while the latter pair refers to those in which the fund share and the contributions are large (*fuerte*) or small (*pequeña*).

As the table indicates, *tanda* appears in northern, central, and southern Mexican states, and is more frequently used than *cundina*. *Cundina*, the second most frequently used term, is restricted to some northern Mexican states and the southwestern United States. For unknown reasons, *quiniela* has taken root in Ciudad Juarez, even though the city is only a few hundred miles away from Chihuahua, where *tanda* is the most popular term. Equally curious is the fact that *vaca* is the preferred term in El Paso, which is directly across the border from Ciudad Juárez. On the other hand, *mutualista*, which has long been a term associated only with funerary associations, is the major term used in Mérida, but *caja de ahorro* is used infrequently. Further research to unravel some of the problems raised, such as the routes of diffusion for each term and the exact point of origin for others, is, of course, indicated.

TYPES

Fuertes *and* Pequeñas

Kurtz and Showman (1978: 67) analytically distinguished regular *tandas* from episodic ones in San Felipe and San Jerónimo, Puebla. The regular *tandas* were organized by one person on a repetitive basis; the episodic *tandas* disbanded after a single cycle. The regular *tandas* were embedded in neighborhoods and composed of long-term residents, whereas the members of episodic *tandas* might consist of peers associated at the place of employment, as well as neighbors and relatives.

Most of our informants distinguished between *tandas fuertes* (strong) and *tandas pequeñas* (small). Strong *tandas* and small *tandas* may occur not only in neighborhoods or places of employment but in familial networks as well. They may be composed of long-term residents, relatives, or coworkers. This research found that all three membership types had both episodic and regular *tandas*. In some long-term *tandas*, the organizer inherited the *tanda* from a previous organizer from the same neighborhood or place of employment, or from a lineal or consanguineous family member. The passing on of *tandas* provides a kind of cultural cement, which generates *confianza* and a legitimacy lacking in episodic or short-term *tandas*. Higher contributions are more likely in strong *tandas* than in small ones. In addition, the dense social relationships between participants in small *tandas* may have accumulated because of their long-term association with the same organizer and other RCA participants. One informant had participated in the same RCA with the same organizer and with about 75 percent of the original membership for over 20 years. Such density can also have been previously generated by multiple ties, such as friendship, fictive kinship, and residence in the same area. In either case such density contributes to the strength and durability of the strong *tandas*.

The small *tandas* are usually organized to meet short-range goals, such as a pressing economic need or a forgotten ritual obligation. These may also consist of people with dense social relationships, but the density of relationships is unlikely to have been generated by *tanda* participation itself. Contributions and the number of participants are likely to be small, since immediate goals must be fulfilled. Strong *tandas* will tend to have characteristics associated with regular *tandas* and small *tandas* characteristics associated with episodic ones.

Informal, Intermediate, and Formal RCAs

The least complex RCA is the informal association in which participants are tied by *confianza* and the associations are embedded within the participants' residential, work, or familial networks and contexts. Sanctions, accounting processes, and contributions and collections are all accomplished face-to-face. Informal associations are of two subtypes, commercialized and noncommercialized. Chapter 2 analyzes them.

A more formal RCA organizationally, but one that can be either commercialized or noncommercialized, is the intermediate RCA in which the contributions and fund share are handled by an accountant or bookkeeper of a company. For example, in Tapachula, the cashier of a small factory is in charge of deducting the *tanda* contribution from a participant's pay. In addition, all members are provided a document showing that they belong to the *tanda* and that they agree to abide by its rules. The cashier keeps a formal record of payments and disbursements. An expanded discussion of this type appears in Chapter 2.

The most complex and formal organizationally are the commercialized *mutualistas* (mutual society) of Yucatán. The *mutualistas* are RCAs run by a corporation licensed by the state of Yucatán. The corporation is responsible for the simultaneous functioning of RCAs of different amounts.

The crucial differences between these RCAs, then, lie in the potential sanctions and the degree of complexity and commercialization: the Mérida *mutualista* is organized by corporations sanctioned by the state, whereas the intermediate RCA is embedded within the accounting system of a private firm but is not organized or formally sanctioned by the firm. It lends its machinery but is not responsible for the operation of the RCA. While records are kept even in the most informal association, it operates with only the moral sanction derived from the *confianza* enjoyed by the organizer vis-à-vis the participants and the participants vis-à-vis each other.

Specialized RCAs

Specialized RCAs have never been reported in the Mexican literature. The Volkswagen and Datsun *tandas* of Mexico City have already been mentioned. Automobile *tandas* may also exist in Puebla. (Puebla is the site of the largest Volkswagen plant in Mexico so that the idea of a Volkswagen *tanda* is certainly plausible, but I have been unable to verify their existence.) In these *tandas* 40 persons contribute 2,200 pesos a month for approximately 40 months. Each month one of the 40 is selected by lottery to be the new Volkswagen or Datsun owner. Regardless of when the person receives his car, he must eventually contribute the total amount of his purchase. It is obvious that the longer the rotational cycle has been in operation, the greater the likelihood of being selected since those having received an automobile are removed from the lottery, although they continue to pay contributions.

House *tandas* work in the same manner, and one of our key informants occupied a house acquired by means of a house *tanda*. In quilt RCAs participants contribute small amounts weekly and receive quilts as the fund shares. These are commercialized RCAs since the organizer is selling the quilts at a profit. The operation is something of a shell game.

There are book RCAs in which elementary schoolchildren contribute money toward the purchase of books which are then rotated by lot to participants. These are begun before the start of the school year among children who attend the same school. The drinking-bout RCAs have already been described. Equally as specialized are the "birthday" *tandas* formed by wealthy matrons who contribute 1,000 pesos a month and purchase birthday gifts for each other with the accumulated contributions. In the same class sector are variants called canasta *tandas*, in which card games are played and the pot is accumulated to purchase gifts. More types, as well as their operational complexity, are described in the following chapters.

Among the more intriguing types are the commuter *cundinas* which operate between Tijuana and the San Diego area. As will be seen in Chapter 5, these are tied to changes in the rate of exchange and the profit-making possibilities these present. There are two kinds of commuter *cundinas*. Some are composed of people who work in San Diego but participate in *cundinas* in Tijuana where they live. The organizer, who usually lives in Tijuana, commutes back and forth across the border, collecting and dispensing money on paydays in San Diego. In the second kind, people organize associations in the San Diego area that include participants from Tijuana. The organizer may live in either Tijuana or San Diego, but for both kinds the rate of exchange between the dollar and the peso is crucial.

It is quite significant that this research has found commercialized RCAs of varying degrees of organizational formality, because the types that Penny (1968), Wu (1974), and Kurtz and Showman (1978) consider most worthy of being designated commercial are the ones they believe are most likely to evolve into the referent models for development as "intermediate" economic institutions. The characteristics they suggest as defining a commercial association are, however, neither necessary or sufficient. I have shown elsewhere (Vélez-Ibañez 1982), that the characteristics that Penny (1968) and Wu (1974) postulate as essential to commercialization—long duration cycles, large sums, charges made for an early fund share—are not crucial. Rather, to denote any rotating credit association as "commercialized," it is only necessary that a specialist or organization of specialists receive remuneration. The literature's failure to develop this definition accounts for the failure to report or analyze fully commercial relations within Mexican and Chicano rotating credit associations (Cope and Kurtz 1980; Kurtz 1973; Kurtz and Showman 1978).

In contradistinction to Kurtz and Showman (1978), we found such commercial aspects in many regions in Mexico as well as in parts of the southwestern United States. If one accepts the argument of modernization theory that such commercial practices can serve to educate people in commercial attitudes (Geertz 1962), then certainly the commercialized RCAs described here would serve that function. Yet the commercialized practices found in this research, as well as the acquisition of commercial attitudes, antedate modernization theories. In fact, the formally organized *mutualista* was a late nineteenth- and early twentieth-century practice, as newspapers of the period demonstrate.[8] Some of our informants had participated in RCAs before modernization notions existed. Two informants placed the beginnings of fee-type *cundinas* of Tijuana-San Diego between 1936 and 1938 while another informant in Mérida had participated in a *mutualista* in 1943. He had been appointed agent in the government department where he worked and was responsible for *mutualistas* in which 365 fellow employees participated. I have already alluded to an informant from the state of Sinaloa whose parents had participated in *cundinas* 60 years prior to this research.

The fact that *mutualistas, cundinas,* and RCAs in general were in existence long before notions of modernization became popular, and that such practices were commercialized, indicates that people had learned to save long before it was thought fashionable, and had in the process learned commercial attitudes as well. These are the very indicators thought important for development and indicate movement toward the very goals developmentalists seem to appreciate most: the dynamic use of funds. Yet long after the first uses of the RCAs, the degree of inequality in the distribution of Mexican income, no matter how it is measured, exceeds that of most of the world's developing countries (Hansen 1971: 83). Mexicans in the United States are badly off economically in relation to non-Mexicans, with 34.7 percent of Mexican families having incomes of $15,000 or more, compared to 54.9 percent of non-Mexican families with incomes of $15,000 or more. But since Mexican families have a mean number of 4.06 persons per family in comparison to 3.31 for non-Mexican families, the comparison is actually even more unfavorable (U.S., Department of Commerce 1979: 13). In addition, non-Mexican figures include the black population, whose removal would increase the mean income of the nonblack, non-Mexican population as well as reduce the number of persons supported by the mean income. Neither for Mexicans in Mexico or in the United States do the rotating credit associations seem to serve as an efficacious mechanism for structural change.

2 The Process and Structure of Operational Cycles

INTRODUCTION

The cross-cultural literature on rotating credit associations basically emphasizes the need for money as the impetus for joining such associations. While such a motive is quite usual among Mexicans, there are also nonindividual stimuli for joining. Just as the Javanese experience a more communal impetus to join rotating credit associations (Geertz 1962: 243), so Mexicans participate for other than economic reasons. Among Mexicans, both the joining and the recruitment processes are related in some degree to the contexts in which rotating credit associations emerge, so that the associations are part of embedded social networks in occupational, residential, and familial contexts. Class dimensions, however, influence both processes.

The basic mechanisms of operation of the associations sampled are generally the same, but permutations are generated by differences in the amount contributed, the number of persons participating, the number of permissible contributions per person, and the amount of time a full cycle of operation takes. The introduction of other variables, such as splitting a single contribution, borrowing money on a share, or introducing political considerations into the decision on the order in which people receive their fund share, increases the complexity of operation. Nevertheless the rotating credit associations sampled in this study show congruence between the number of persons participating, the amount of the fund shares, and the duration of the rotation cycle.

JOINING AND RECRUITMENT

The manner in which RCAs begin is related to their contexts. Some, like episodic associations, begin spontaneously. People form these when they are hard pressed to pay a debt or want to accumulate cash to make an investment or buy a major consumer good. The initiator will usually ask co–workers, relatives, friends, and neighbors to join a new association. Each person asked may ask another to join even though the organizer does not know him or her. In any case, the willingness to establish *confianza* must exist prior to the actual establishment of the RCA. *Confianza* can be based on longevity of employment or the age of the person, or it may have been established in other ways. Participants do not establish the same degree of *confianza* with all members, but a minimum of *confianza* is expected between the organizer and the participants and among some of the participants. *Confianza* then expands to all other participants through various links. *Confianza* links will be both direct and indirect and will vary in quality and density. In many cases, members must trust in the trust of others to complete their obligations, since they know little about them. As one informant put it, "Mutual trust is lent."

Some RCA organizers have an established reputation. They have organized or participated in associations that have lasted up to 15 years. (Fifteen years is unusually long and in this particular case was attributable to the large number of people who participated.) In some RCAs a continuous membership is maintained; these tend to be characterized by allotments of more than one share per person, a membership of fewer than 20 people, and the involvement of a full-time organizer. The organizer in such a case will be marked by prestigious characteristics besides those associated with the RCA, such as age, reputation, and political relationships. Some regularized *tandas* have been inherited through friendship or consanguineous relations, and the founder's reputation is passed on to the new organizer. In such cases the ritual introduction of the new organizer is made by the old one. The new organizer is taken to each household for an extended visit, and formal introductions are made over some commensal activity. After the introductions have been completed, the new organizer holds a dinner for the participants and the old organizer, at which time *confianza* and the new organizer's reputation are ritually sealed.

In contrast, some associations have been turned over to an individual by the participants who organized them, because they cannot settle on whom they wish to be responsible for collecting money, keeping records, allocating numbers, and dispersing the fund. In one case, this person was the only female participant who came from the same home town as the other participants. The males could not agree among themselves, but saw the only woman as the person of greatest *confianza* since there seemed to be a covert understanding that women were generally trustworthy.

RCAs, however, can also be generated as part of larger complex reciprocal relations originating in familial, friendship, institutional, or residential contexts. The RCA is an economic extension of other dense relations, like those reported by Lomnitz (1977: 131–158), but it develops in other contexts as well. Such intense interactive networks appear, for example, among female government office workers who combine ritual gift giving, commensal activities, and economic assistance. The origins of their exchange complexes, of which the RCA is a crucial reciprocal mechanism, lie not in subsistence needs as reported by Lomnitz, or in the drives of individual organizers. Instead, the total complex of dense relations among these office workers provides the impetus for the establishment of a regular method of distributing money. These are "normal social relations" (Goffman 1961: 6) replicated within such partial institutions as government or private corporate organizations.

These institutional RCAs are of interest since they are organized by the participants themselves. The person responsible for collecting the contribution is the person whose turn it is to receive the fund share, not an organizer. Therefore the rotation, the collection, and the dispensing of money are cooperatively accomplished, but tied to ritual gift giving (birthdays, feast days, and saints' days) and eating together donated pies and cakes during lunch hours. Three levels of exchange emerge: the RCA, gift giving, and eating together. Each is not necessarily related to subsistence needs. *Confianza*, nevertheless, is also reinforced and expressed through such activities.

Even among commercial RCAs, however, *confianza* is an important means of entrée. For example, in one of the border cities, an organizer is responsible for strictly upper-middle-class *cundinas* of $1,000, in which 10 persons contribute $25 weekly plus a 10 percent fee over a period of 44 weeks. The fee amounts to $25 dollars weekly (10% × 25 = $2.50 × 10 persons = $25) and is placed in reserve in case one of the participants, for whatever reasons, cannot contribute the amount agreed upon. Even with this reserve fund as a cushion, the organizer usually does not allow anyone to enter the various *cundinas* she controls without already having established *confianza* relationships. In five *cundinas* sampled, which included 50 persons, only 8 persons were relatively "new," and the rest were long-term participants. This particular organizer recruited solely from the upper-middle-class social networks, to which she gained access through her membership in various voluntary service clubs (see "Contexts and Sectors," Chapter 3, for more details).

CLASS DIMENSIONS

Most organizers indicated that no invitation is extended to persons whose statuses are not fixed either occupationally, residentially, consanguinously, fictively, affinally, or by friendship. Yet many people are at first reluctant to join because they know about savings accounts or harbor doubts about the validity of the rotation process, and the organizer must overcome this resistance. The organizer's success is based on establishing *confianza* and on his status and does not depend on the newcomer establishing *confianza* with the other participants. There are class specific stimuli that encourage people to participate in the RCAs.

Working-class and economically marginal persons who agreed to join often contrasted RCAs to formal institutions such as banks or savings and loan offices. Persons interviewed stated that while formal institutions demanded intimate knowledge ("everything in one's life from top to bottom"), no reciprocal personal relationships were generated. Mutuality was absent in commercial relations. On the other hand, *confianza* in the associations was made up of intimate personal knowledge and a public reputation, and was privately secured in established personal relationships of trust. Since intimate knowledge and personal relationships are the basic ingredients of *confianza* that generate mutual trust, formal institutions were in fact the antithesis of the informal rotating credit associations for these populations.

In other words, for the RCA, personal relations must exist, and the needed personal information is already known. On the other hand, for public institutions personal relations are unwanted, whereas personal information, although needed, is unknown.

While either a joiner's or an organizer's reputation is public knowledge within the networks people join or are recruited from, the reputation exists and is usually interlocked within limited private social domains. Thus the necessary personal information forms the basis of the reputation of the person invited or wishing to join an RCA. From this information the personal relations between joiners and organizers are matched to form the basis of *confianza*, which glues the joiner to the organizer. On the other hand, public institutions have no privately generated reputations within limited private social domains, and the relations generated in those domains are primarily "single-stranded" types (Boissevain 1974: 30) in which persons engage in a single role relation like that between a bank officer and a depositor or borrower. Yet for those in working-class and marginal sectors an inherent contradiction exists. Such institutions need personal information from clients to justify the establishment of a single-stranded relationship for market purposes, yet they demand this information without expressing such an exchange on a personal level. There is, in other words, no *confianza* established.

These, however, are the initial dynamics occurring when those in working-class or marginal sectors join RCAs. How the members *use* their money once it is accumulated is another question. Once they have built up sufficient capital to open an account in which personal data are required without personal embarrassment, many RCA participants seem to regard themselves as sufficiently "respectable" to enter into market exchange relations with public institutions. Much more is said in the discussion on the use of money in the last section of this chapter. Nevertheless, it should be pointed out here that for these classes and sectors money is necessary to establish a reputation. For middle- and upper-class sectors, who can if they wish become part of traditional banking or savings institutions, the impetus to join is not the same.

Within middle-class sectors, men and women frequently live beyond their means. The purchase of an automobile at high interest rates, private school tuition, the limitations imposed by a single income, the buying of a fashionable home, and the recreational activities standard in such sectors, place very real strains on inflation-ridden budgets.[1] These people find it difficult to maintain class-specific expectations without relatively large amounts of money. An RCA, because it sets up an obligatory savings scheme within the same class network and does not require any (already committed) collateral, may provide a desirable way to have access to funds at regular intervals. Informants suggested that the pressures to consume or to pay debts immediately made it almost impossible to save, but that the RCAs are a scheme of *forced* savings that circumvents an individual's desire to spend already committed funds. Such saving takes place within the context of other relations of *confianza*, and the threat of losing prestige if obligations are unmet reinforces the stability of the RCA.

The forced savings aspect was repeatedly mentioned by all classes, but especially by the middle classes. They seem more prone to living beyond their means, and the importance of the RCAs is related to this factor more than to values of thriftiness.

Since the upper-middle-class and some upper-class sectors have ready access to resources, and profit-making ventures, the RCAs do not serve as forced-saving vehicles for them. Among some women in upper-middle- or upper-class residential areas, the associations are a means by which to enter prestigious residential networks. Thus, in the wealthy residential area of the Lomas de Chapultepec of Mexico City a 15-woman network uses the associations to screen newly arrived residents. Embedded within commensal, gift-giving, and card-playing activities, RCAs are used as recruiting mechanisms. The high cost of the contributions, 1,000 pesos per month, indicates status and a willingness to share with other women on the same economic level. Usually, such contributions are not reallocated by lot or by chronology but are spent on luxury birthday gifts for each of the women. Over a period of three to six months, between 45,000 and 90,000 pesos are accumulated, so that the elaborate birthday gifts can be purchased. Since some of the 15 women will have been born in the same month, special efforts are made to include women whose dates of birth are not too close to others. Therefore, no more than 7 persons will have their birthdays during a six-month period so that each gift will be worth approximately 12,000 pesos. Here the emphasis is less on the worth of the gift than on the imagination shown in its purchase. "Sumptuous consumption" and network recruitment, not balanced scarcity or spending beyond one's means, are the primary motives for joining RCAs.

Among lawyers, doctors, businessmen, and other professionals, high-stakes associations are common, even though all are familiar with savings institutions and other forms of interest-bearing investments. These RCAs, in which the worth of the fund share is 150,000 pesos, are usually part of larger voluntary associations, such as a Chamber of Commerce or the International Lion's Club. Each member contributes 10,000 pesos per month in a 15-member *cundina*. Heads of bureaucracies and even corporate officers of banking institutions and economic planning offices also participate in RCAs. Here, clearly, such cooperative activities are not initiated because of economic need, or because the members live beyond their means. Nor do they reflect a desire for sumptuous consumption. Rather, political stresses placed on individuals within the various social domains in which their professional activities take place select for RCA participation, as further analysis will illustrate.

In addition, retired elderly upper-middle-class cosmopolitans have formed associations as part of their recreational activities, such as playing canasta, giving parties, going on excursions, and attending recreational painting classes. Here the impetus for joining RCAs does not lie in a scarcity of resources, the members living beyond their means, their desire for sumptuous consumption, or political stresses, but instead the desire to fill the final days of the life cycle.

BASIC MECHANISMS AND STRUCTURES

As has been stated, the structures and mechanisms involved in the Mexican RCAs vary in complexity. Among the simplest is the leaderless one with a small contribution and fund share. It is socially dense and cooperatively run, occupational or residential, with neither a part-time nor full-time specialist. In such an RCA, the basic mechanism is as follows: usually 5 to 10 persons agree to form the RCA and decide the amount to be contributed, how often the money is to be collected—weekly, semi-monthly, or monthly, depending on the source of income—and how often the money is to be allocated. In private corporations in both Mexico and the United States weekly contributions tend to be the norm, with semimonthly or monthly contributions usual in public corporations or government offices. For example, 5 restaurant service workers at the Beverly Hills Hotel in Los Angeles were paid semimonthly at a rate of $75. Four would contribute a semimonthly paycheck to the current recipient of the fund share. After drawing paper slips marked from one to five, number 1 would be designated to receive $300 at the first turn. The following month number 2 would receive the amount, and so on until four months after the first turn when all five would have received $300, and the rotation would be complete.

Participants in simple RCAs do not necessarily contribute their whole salary. Often the contributions are smaller, and can be as low as the equivalent of $2.25 in pesos RCAs and $25 in dollar RCAs. Nor do contributions and the allocation of fund shares have to occur at the same time. Contributions can be made weekly and the fund share allocated monthly.

In the simple RCAs two intervening factors play important parts in defining the complexity of operation: the number and class sector of participants. Most simple RCAs without a leader contained 10 persons, and the amounts contributed were relatively small with no fees or interest charges. In most residential and occupational sectors of working-class or marginal populations such RCAs were common. Similar RCAs of about the same size but in which large amounts were rotated occur among high-level managers and professionals. Thus within a national government agency in Mexico responsible for economic agricultural forecasting, a 1,000-peso contribution for a 10,000-peso rotation was operated without a leader by 10 economists, geographers, rural sociologists, and demographers. The glue of *confianza* in this case had been established among 5 of the 10, who had attended the same preparatory school, and university classes, and had been students of the same internationally famous Mexican economist. The other 5 had varying degrees of *confianza* among these friends.

In both the Beverly Hills example and the economic planning agency, participation was relatively closed according to class and occupation. In these two examples of the simplest RCA we see both large and small contributions, but common to both were the dense social relations generated between participants. Therefore, two factors must be kept in mind in considering the complexity of the informal RCA: those with fewer persons will have fewer organizational problems of control or difficulties in collecting and dispensing money since *confianza* is the primary vehicle for all participants; and second, the number of persons and their class sector will determine the frequency of collection, as well as the probable working out of the total cycle. An operation will be much more complex in a working-class R C A in which contributions are made on a payment plan, with records to be kept, accounts to be maintained, and interest to be charged for tardy payments. On the other hand, persons with resources are generally not going to pay on a payment plan, and the collection of money is certainly much simpler.

Permutations

Permutations emerge, however, with variations in the amount contributed, the number of persons participating, the number of contributions allowed, and the duration of a full cycle. In one such permutation in Ciudad Netzahualcoyótl, 30 turns worth 100 pesos each were made available to *six* contributing persons. Membership was thus restricted. Those who participated selected as many turns as they could afford. Thus one person selected turns 1–10, another 11–15, another 16–20, two others 21–25 and 26–29, and one person turn 30. For 30 weeks an exchange of money occurred with the fund for each person ranging from 2,900 pesos to 20,000 pesos. Person 1 had selected turns 1–10, each worth 100 pesos, and contributed 1,000 pesos weekly. Person 2 selected turns 11–15 and contributed 500 pesos weekly. Person 3 with turns 16–20 and person 4 with turns 21–25 also each contributed 500 pesos weekly. Person 5 selected turns 26–29 and contributed 400 pesos weekly. Finally, person 6 with turn 30 contributed only 100 pesos each week.

Person 1 who had the first 10 turns did not pay but only received during the first 10 weeks. Beginning with the 11th week, the first person paid 1,000 pesos a week, which is equal to 100 times the number of shares he requested, until the end of the rotation of all members. Person 2 who had turns 11–15 paid person 1 500 pesos a week for the first 10 weeks; person 3 who had turns 16–20 paid person 1 500 pesos a week for the first 10 weeks; person 4 who had turns 21–25 paid person 1 500 pesos for the first 10 weeks; person 5 who had turns 26–29 paid person 1 400 pesos a week for the first 10 weeks; and the last person who had only the 30th turn paid person 1 100 pesos a week for the first 10 weeks. Thus person 1 received 2,000 pesos a week from the other 5 in the *tanda* for 10 weeks for a total of 20,000 pesos.

After the tenth week, person 2 who had turns 11–15 began to receive money: from person 1, who had 10 turns (1–10), 1,000 pesos a week for 5 weeks; from person 3 who had 5 turns (16–20) 500 pesos a week for 5 weeks; from person 4 who had 5 turns (21–25) 500 pesos a week for 5 weeks; from person 5 who had 4 turns (26–29) 400 pesos a week for 5 weeks; and from person 6 who had 1 turn (30) 100 pesos a week for 5 weeks. Thus person 2 received 2,500 pesos a week from the other 5 members for 5 weeks for a total of 12,500 pesos.

Persons 3 and 4 went through exactly the same process as person 2, being paid the same total weekly since they also held 5 turns. In each case they received 2,500 pesos weekly for a total of 12,500 pesos. After person 4 had received her turn, 25 weeks had elapsed.

Person 5 who had 4 turns (26–29), received 2,600 pesos for 4 weeks: 1,000 a week from person 1, 500 a week from persons 2, 3, and 4, and 100 pesos a week from person 6. This totals 10,400 pesos for the 4-week period, and the elapsed time was 29 weeks. Person 6 who had turn 30 received one lump sum of 2,900 pesos at the end of the *tanda*. In each case no person received more than what she or he had contributed. (See Appendix A.)

The number of possible permutations for this sort of informal RCA is quite large, and many versions of it are common, especially among persons who have not only a qualitative relationship of density but also one of long duration. On the other hand, there are commercialized informal RCAs exactly like the one just described, which operate in the same way, but add to each weekly contribution a 10 percent fee for the organizer. Thus each person contributes more than what he or she receives. In the example just discussed, the last individual would pay 110 pesos weekly for a total of 3,190 pesos but receive only 2,900 from the rest of the association members. The organizer's earnings would be 10 percent of the total contributions paid (10% of 70,800, or 7,080 pesos).

Other versions of the simply organized RCA whose mechanisms determine the amount of money to be rotated include those in which disbursement is delayed so that fund shares increase. Thus, for example, 10 persons will contribute 1,000 pesos per week for 5 weeks. In the fifth week one person is allocated 50,000 pesos (10 persons × 1,000 pesos × 5 weeks = 50,000 pesos) and every fifth week thereafter, one person will receive 50,000 pesos. The cycle of collection and allocation thus takes 50 weeks. It is not rare for 10-week extensions to occur so that among a 10-person *tanda* of this sort, 100,000 pesos would be allocated every tenth week for a total cycle of 100 weeks. The allocation period can also be shortened. In one case the amount contributed was enlarged so that in a 30,000-peso fund, 10 persons collected and received all the money in 90 days.

The exchange mechanisms can be complicated by participants doubling or splitting their shares, exchanging numbers, or borrowing against the share fund. If such variations have not been previously agreed to, it is more than likely that intense local-level political hassles will ensue. Negotiations to alter the mechanisms of the RCA will generate a host of claims and counterclaims between the organizer and the participants. In those RCAs in which it is understood that such alterations are possible, the political maneuvering will take place before the operations begin. In both cases local-level political struggles may be intensified, as the RCA evolves under changing circumstances and unforeseen factors, which create uncertainty for organizers and participants.

This can be clearly seen in the informal RCA in which there is an organizer, but in which no objective mechanism like a lottery is used to determine the order of turns. Instead, old favors are cashed in, claims of proximity made, and feelings played upon. In those informal RCAs in which the order of turns is negotiated intense political claims and counterclaims emerge. For example, an organizer may save the first turns for close relatives or friends and inform all other participants that those turns are taken, or the organizer may claim to have taken the first turn and then negotiate for that first turn with someone else shortly before the beginning of the RCA cycle. When fellow participants learn of such intrigues, feelings will be hurt and further claims will be made against both the organizer and the person for whom the favor was done. A series of incidents similar in quality to the ethnodrama in Chapter 4 will then ensue.[2]

For those who have participated in RCAs with the same organizer for a number of years, seniority determines who is to receive the first turn. Thus a person may have begun with turn 16 in her or his first RCA and, after having participated in 13 RCAs, be given the opportunity to select turn 3 in a new RCA. However, even long-standing participants often claim greater seniority in order to receive the turn sooner. Thus it is extremely important to keep records.

On the other hand, the organizer may understate one participant's seniority in order to give someone else with greater *confianza* an earlier turn. In such cases the organizer sometimes gives her or his own first turn to the long-standing participant and gives the other contested turn to the person with greater *confianza* or vice versa. However, if the former strategy is followed much more intense political problems with the long-standing participant will follow since he or she will claim one of the first turns in the next RCA. In either case, the selection of turns in formal RCAs can be made much more complicated by the introduction of intense local-level politics.

Intermediate and Formal Structures

Although intermediate RCAs and the formal institutionalized *mutualistas* are also subject to local-level political maneuvering, both types operate relatively consistently and their mechanisms remain largely unchanged. The intermediate RCAs are relatively stable because they are set within the context of a formal accounting system, in, for example, a factory, a bureau office, or a service company. The turns are selected only once, contributions are deducted through the payroll, a written agreement of participation is included, and the turns and the shares allotted are recorded. One must remember the distinction between RCAs that are formally integrated into a company's accounting system and those that only use the accounting system to keep the RCA records. An informally organized RCA can become a management-controlled association when conflict over the mechanisms of the RCA leads the management to "take over" the RCA from the employees. In the latter type, the bookkeeper or accountant is the organizer or a prominent member, but the company's accounting system is used without managerial sanction. In such cases the accounting practices are impressive, since three sets of books are kept: one for the company, one for RCA members, and one for the accountant.

The formally organized *mutualistas* of Mérida are the most

complex of all the RCAs. In the most commercialized, *confianza* has been replaced by collateral. Anyone wishing to join such an association must agree to a lien over movable or unmovable property. The central mechanism is the market exchange one, so that only those with enough accumulated property are eligible to join.

The bodies responsible for the transactions of the *mutualistas* are corporations with officers and other formal institutional characteristics. While fund shares vary from 20,000 to 150,000 pesos (10,000-peso shares were discontinued in 1978), the structural elements and processes are the same in all of them. Each new *mutualista* is usually announced in the local newspapers which describe the amount of the "savings fund" (*fondos de ahorro*); the number of shares (*acciones*); their individual worth; the duration of the total cycle; the age restrictions (15–60); the legal sponsor (the corporation); and the objective (obligatory savings). Each person is required to sign a lien equal to the amount of the advertised fund share. Each person provides an initial deposit and fee which varys with the amount of the fund share and in addition signs a contract of agreement (Appendix B). In return the person receives a certificate of participation and association and insurance against death or permanent disability during the life of the *mutualista*.

At the beginning cycle of the *mutualista*, each person is given a number registered solely in her or his name. That number will be on one of the 40 or 50 (depending on the number of participants) lottery balls placed in a large wire hopper. Every 10 weeks, the winning numbers are randomly selected. The lottery process shifts according to computational tables, as fewer and fewer persons continue to be eligible. The frequency of sorting increases as the number of persons participating decreases. A new cycle of operation begins when 50 other persons are registered as members. As a result three or four months may pass between the end of one *mutualista* and the beginning of a new one. Because of the difference in amounts (20,000 to 150,000 pesos) four and five *mutualistas* may operate simultaneously on different cycles with an entirely different set of people participating in each one.

The terms for payment and receipt of money are more complicated than this description would suggest. Those selected first during the course of the cycle in fact pay more than they receive for the privilege of using the money first. Those whose numbers are selected last pay less than what they receive as compensation for allowing others the use of their money.

To see how a *mutualista* works consider a 20,000-peso, 40-person *mutualista*. Each individual pays an initial contribution of 54 pesos for 326 weeks. After the person has received his or her 20,000 pesos, a premium of 26 pesos is added weekly for an 80-peso total. The person selected first in the lottery pays 80 pesos weekly for 326 weeks for a total of 26,080 pesos. The twentieth person pays 54 pesos for the first 163 weeks, and a premium of 26 pesos for the next 163 weeks for a total of 21,842 pesos. The fortieth person pays only 54 pesos for 326 weeks for a total of 17,604 pesos. The totals include interest charges not computed in these figures, so that each total in fact is greater than the figures given here. All participants will *receive* at least 20,000 pesos, the amount originally agreed to by all participants.

At this complex level of operation the *mutualista*, by making its investors' funds available for use by others, functions exactly like a commercial lending and borrowing institution. The crucial difference between *mutualistas* and traditional savings and loan institutions is the lottery, which determines whether a person will be a lender or a borrower. This element of chance is of course entirely absent in the usual savings and loan institution.

As in commercial institutions, the lenders' and borrowers' funds are used to maintain the organizational structure of the corporation, including the overhead costs of the *mutualistas*. These are calculated at 6 percent of each payment made. Eight percent of the fund share is allocated for "collection and administration," which includes salaries to the collectors who ride out daily on their motorcycles to gather payments; rent and utilities; supplies and materials; and the salaries of fiscal and corporate accountants.

These costs include honorariums for the corporate officers. In one corporation, the officers receiving salaries and honorariums included the president of the *mutualista*, who was the corporation secretary's son; the secretary, who was the president's mother; and the director-treasurer who was the secretary's brother and the president's uncle. It would seem that *confianza*, while excluded between the corporation and *mutualista* participants, was in fact highly valued within the corporate organization.

BASIC CHARACTERISTICS OF THE ROTATING CREDIT ASSOCIATIONS: THE SAMPLE

Number of Participants

Of the 90 formal, intermediate, and informal RCAs sampled in which money is the medium of exchange, 80 are informally organized residential, occupational, familial, or friendship types, both commercialized and noncommercialized. Data have been collected on 5 intermediate RCAs that are formally or informally integrated into the accounting system of companies, and on one formal corporation (Mutualista de Yucatán, a pseudonym) and its 5 *mutualistas*. The various specialized RCAs are excluded except for a brief mention of VW *tandas*. Not all the discussions will reflect all 90 RCAs, only those for which the data are complete and reliable will be used, so that the total number of RCAs will vary with the specific topic being considered.

The categories of informal, intermediate, and formal are used as convenient distinctions. "Peso" and "dollar" refers to the currency used in the associations, but it should be understood that this does not automatically indicate the physical location of the association, since many RCAs in Mexican border states use dollars as the medium of exchange. The opposite, however, does not occur. The use of pesos in U.S. RCAs has never been reported.

Figure 2.1 illustrates the frequency of the number of persons engaged in informal and intermediate associations.

In the 65 RCAs analyzed, 10-person RCAs were most frequent, 12- and 20-person RCAs next most frequent, and 5- and 15-person RCAs third most frequent. An assorted number of persons participated in others with the same or slightly different frequency. The Volkswagen or Datsun RCAs have a maximum of around 40 persons. More participants would certainly extend the period in which the VWs and Datsuns could be allotted and counterbalance the advantages of such RCAs.

As can be seen in Figure 2.1, informal and intermediate RCAs of 10 persons occur twice as often as those of 12 and 20, and slightly more than six times as often as those of 5 and 15 persons.

Figure 2.1. Number of Participants in Informal and Intermediate RCAs

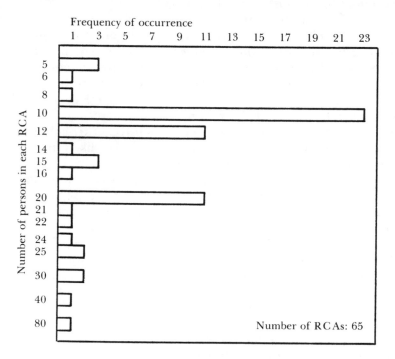

This indicates that 10-person RCAs are the preferred size for informal and intermediate types. Care must be taken in making such a generalization, however, since many RCAs have 11 or 12 persons or fewer than 10, depending on circumstances. Nevertheless, the evidence seems to indicate that the 10-person RCA is more manageable; it corresponds to a relatively short period (usually 10 months), and increases the probability that *confianza* has been established among the participants. Having only 10 participants reduces the distance traveled by an organizer in residential RCAs, and 10 probably corresponds closely to the maximum number of colleagues with friendship ties in an office, factory, or business concern. With 10 participants the certainty that funds will be properly allocated increases, since some of the participants will be

part of other networks of relationships. It is more likely that with
10 persons, a larger portion of the participants will have developed multiple relations than in larger RCAs.

For the formally organized *mutualistas* of Yucatán, the information on membership size was gathered from one corporation.
According to the corporation, most *mutualistas* are composed of
50 persons if the fund share is worth 50,000 pesos or more and
40 persons if it is worth 20,000 pesos or less. Of the 5 *mutualistas* for which there is reliable information, 3 have 50 participants and 2 have 40. The corporate officers were reluctant to
disclose the exact number of persons in each RCA. If, however,
an average size of 45 is assumed, it is more than likely that in
fact at least 44 *mutualistas* were in operation within this corporation at the time this research was carried out, since more than
2,000 persons were reported to be engaged in them. (These remarks concern only the Mutualista de Yucatán and not any other
corporation.)

My data agree with Kurtz's (1973) and Kurtz and Showman's
(1978) findings for San Ysidro, San Felipe, and San Jerónimo that
10-person memberships in informal RCAs are common. But
Kurtz and Showman also report membership sizes ranging from 3
to 26 in San Felipe and San Jerónimo and Lomnitz (1977: 88)
reports groups of 4 to 10. I found no informal RCA with less
than 5 or as many as 26 members.

My findings conflict with Kurtz and Showman's suggestion that
there is "no necessary correspondence between the number of
memberships and number of members" (1978: 67). There are in-
dications that in the more commercialized informal RCAs directed by specialists, care is taken to limit the number of memberships to the number of members, for reasons of organizational
convenience. In formally organized *mutualistas* this is certainly
the case, and no more people than shares available were recorded.
In those associations that do not have a specialist or charge a fee
it is probable that much more variation between the number of
memberships and the number of participants will occur. In this
sense, Kurtz and Showman are perfectly correct in their findings
since their research did not uncover commercialized informal
RCAs of the intermediate sort or the formal corporate-directed
mutualista.

Amounts Contributed

The sums contributed in informal and intermediate peso RCAs varied from 50 to 10,000 pesos. Thirty percent of the associations had contributions of 100 pesos; 28 percent contributions of 50 pesos; 19 percent contributions of 200–300 pesos; 13 percent contributions of 600–1,000 pesos; 7 percent contributions of 350–500 pesos; finally, 1 percent had contributions of 2,000 and 1 percent contributions of 3,000–10,000. Figure 2.2 shows the frequency distribution in percentages.

The sums contributed in the informal and intermediate dollar RCAs show a range of $25–100. The modal contribution was $50 and accounted for 35 percent of the associations; $100 contributions were next most frequent (30 percent of the RCAs); 26 percent had $25 contributions which was the lowest amount among dollar RCAs; and last, 4 percent of the associations had contributions of $30 and 4 percent contributions of $75. Figure 2.3 shows the frequency distribution.

A comparison of the frequency distributions for peso and dollar RCAs shows an interesting difference when the amounts are converted to corresponding amounts in the other currency

Figure 2.2. Sums Contributed in Informal and Intermediate Peso RCAs

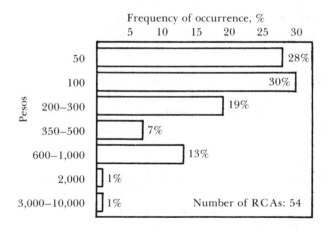

Figure 2.3. Sums Contributed in Informal and Intermediate
Dollar RCAs

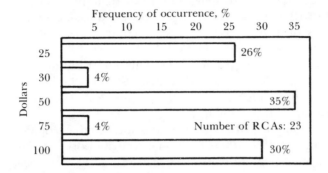

(see Figure 2.4). The most frequent amount in the dollar RCAs
is equivalent to 1,125 pesos (exchange rate of 1979), which is the
third most frequent amount in the peso RCAs (600–1,000). The
second most frequent amount of $100 is comparable to 2,250
pesos which is one of the least frequent amounts in the
peso RCAs.

In comparing the size of the contributions, one finds that the
lowest peso amount is one-tenth of the lowest dollar amount:
$2.25 (equivalent to 50 pesos) compared to $25. There is a wider
spread at the low end of the peso amounts than there is in the
dollar RCAs. In the peso RCAs 84 percent of the RCAs involve
contributions of under $22. (This is computed by adding all
the percentages for peso equivalents of $22 or less, that is, 28, 30,
19, and 7; see Figure 2.4.) On the other hand, as can be seen from
Figure 2.4, dollar RCAs of $25 account for 26 percent of the
contributions.

Thirteen percent of the peso RCAs involve contributions in the
middle range between $27 and $45. On the other hand, in the
dollar RCAs, 39 percent involve contributions between $30 and
$50. While these comparisons between peso and dollar RCAs
cannot be exact, they do tell us something about the differences
between the two types.

Among the higher sums, only 2 percent of the peso RCAs had
contributions between $89 and $445. In the dollar RCAs, 34 percent fall between $75 and $100. It is interesting, however, that
the highest dollar amount in the dollar RCAs is $34–345 lower

Figure 2.4. Comparison of Contributions in Peso and Dollar
Informal and Intermediate RCAs

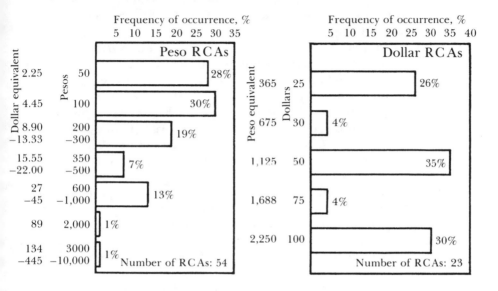

than the highest peso amounts. (This is computed by subtracting
the highest dollar amount of $100 from the highest peso equiva-
lent of $134–445.) What this indicates is that a wider range of
income level participates in peso RCAs than in dollar RCAs.
Wealthier Mexicans are more likely to participate in RCAs in
Mexico than in the United States.

There are great differences in the low and middle ranges between peso and dollar RCAs as well. Eighty-four percent of the
peso RCAs involve contributions of under $22, but only 26 per-
cent of the dollar RCAs involve contributions of less than $25.
The greater frequency of large sums in dollar RCAs and of small
sums in peso RCAs reflects the fact that in border areas, where
dollars are widely used in RCAs, family incomes are among the
highest in the Mexican republic. Incomes are appreciably higher
among Mexicans in the U.S. Southwest as well. Members of the
working class and the upper middle or upper class participate in
dollar RCAs. The $50 amounts appear in 35 percent of the asso-
ciations and are likely to come from workers in the United States,
who are employed in ceramic factories, or in electronic assembly

lines in Los Angeles or San Diego. On the other hand, the $100 amounts, which appear in 30 percent of the dollar RCAs, are more than likely those of professional upper-middle-class men and women of the border states of Baja California, Chihuahua, and Nuevo León.

My data here agree with those of Kurtz and Showman (1978). They found that the sum each person committed to informal peso RCAs, in San Felipe and San Jerónimo normally varied between 50 and 200 pesos. My data (Figure 2.2) show 77 percent of the sums falling between 50 and 300 pesos. Kurtz and Showman, however, do not report any contributions larger than 200 pesos, whereas Figure 2.2 shows that in my study 22 percent (7% + 13% + 1% + 1% = 22%) of the RCAs involve contributions between 350 and 10,000 pesos.

A much greater discrepancy between my data and Kurtz's (1973) occurs with the dollar RCAs. Kurtz's study shows a $5–100 range, with a "norm" of contributions in the $5–10 range (52). My data shows a range of $25 to $100 with three almost evenly distributed "norms" of $25, $50 and $100 (see Figure 2.3). The $50 contributions came from working-class sectors and the $100 amounts from professional sectors, indicating that the populations from which we gathered our information were quite different.

Kurtz's data came solely from an economically marginal population of San Ysidro, whereas mine drew on working-class and professional sectors as well. Furthermore, his research was conducted 10 years before mine. My informants, for example, stated that they had contributed $5 amounts in 1963, and one informant stated that she had contributed such an amount in 1936. Inflation had, however, made the $5 contribution obsolete by 1979 when my research was carried out in the San Diego-Tijuana area.

In the formally organized *mutualistas* of Yucatán, the range of contributions was of course defined by the corporation. Table 2.1 shows five *mutualistas* categorized according to the number of persons involved, the sums contributed, and the fund share allotted.

It must be remembered that the actual amount of the contribution will vary according to each individual's luck in the lottery. The first person selected in the 150,000-peso, 393-week *mutualista* will always pay 320 + 190; the twenty-fifth person will pay 320 pesos for the first 25 turns and 320 + 190 pesos for the next

Table 2.1. *Mutualistas* of Yucatán

Number of Persons	Contribution (in pesos)	Number of Weeks	Fund Share (in thousands of pesos)
50	320 + 190	393	150
50	212 + 128	394	100
50	106 + 64	394	50
40	54 + 26	327	20
40	27 + 13	327	10

Source: Vélez-Ibañez 1982.

25 turns; and the fiftieth person will only pay 320 pesos throughout the 50 turns of the RCA. This scheme of contributions is followed in all the other *mutualistas* in Table 2.1 except that the contributions vary according to the amount of the fund share and the number of persons participating.

Size of Fund Shares

The size of the fund shares differed significantly between peso and dollar RCAs but was of course related to the sums contributed. Figure 2.5 shows that 23 percent of the peso RCAs had fund shares between 500 and 1,000 pesos. Sixteen percent of the peso RCAs had fund shares between 1,100 and 2,000 pesos. RCAs with fund shares between 4,100 and 5,000 pesos accounted for 11 percent of the RCAs. Sizable fund shares of between 9,100 pesos and 150,000 appeared in 24 percent of the RCAs. Fund shares ranged from a low of 200 pesos to a high of 150,000 pesos.

Among the dollar RCAs, fund shares varied from $50 to $10,000. The modal amount lay between $1,000 and $1,250 and was present in 49 percent of the RCAs. Fifteen percent of the dollar RCAs had fund shares of $250. RCAs with fund shares of $50, $300, and $500 appear with a frequency of 8 percent each, while RCAs with $375, $1,500, and $10,000 appear with a frequency of 4 percent each. Figure 2.6 presents these frequencies.

When the peso and dollar RCA funds are compared, the same pattern of income differences emerges as with contributions. The lowest amount in the dollar RCAs ($50) appears in 8 percent of

Figure 2.5. Size of Fund Shares in Informal and
Intermediate Peso RCAs

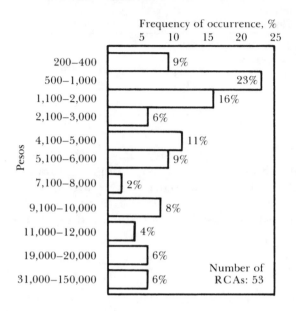

Frequency of occurrence, %

the associations while the lowest amounts in the peso RCAs,
$8.88–$17.00 (converted at the 1979 exchange rate) appear in 9
percent of the associations. The lowest dollar fund shares are 5.6
times as large as the lowest peso fund shares of $8.88 and almost
three times as large as the $17 ones. This shows of course that
those participating in dollar RCAs rotate much larger fund shares,
even at the lowest levels.

Peso RCAs most frequently rotate fund shares worth between
$22 and $44 (converted), an amount considerably smaller than
the amounts most frequently rotated in dollar RCAs ($1,000–
$1,250). Again, differences in income are probably responsible
for this variation.

Six percent of the peso RCAs had fund shares worth between
$844 and $888 (converted) while 49 percent of the dollar RCAs
fall between $1,000 and $1,250. There were no peso RCAs in
exactly that dollar range, but 6 percent of the peso associations
did rotate between $1,377 and $6,667 (converted), which were
the highest fund shares found in informal or intermediate peso

Figure 2.6. Size of Fund Shares in Informal and Intermediate
Dollar RCAs

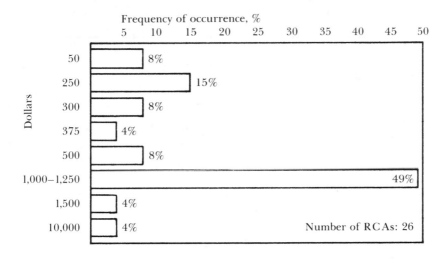

RCAs. The highest fund shares rotated in dollar RCAs were
$10,000, rotated in 4 percent of the associations; 4 percent of the
associations rotated $1,500. Figure 2.7 compares the frequency
distributions of associations by size of fund share.

It is difficult to compare these data to Kurtz and Showman's
(1978), since they do not present theirs in the same way. They
do, however, mention that in San Felipe and San Jerónimo RCAs
the contributions varied from 50 to 200 pesos with a membership
of from 3 to 26 persons and a relatively short cycle (670). Extract-
ing from these data a median contribution of 125 pesos and a
median of 15 (14.5) participants, then it is likely that Kurtz and
Showman's fund shares rotated approximately 1,875 pesos (125
pesos × 15 persons). This is in the range of the second most frequent amount in my data: 1,100–2,000 pesos (accounting for 16%
of the associations). But Kurtz and Showman's median is higher
than my model value of 500–1,000 pesos (accounting for 23% of
the associations). Such comparisons are, of course, very tentative,
since Kurtz and Showman's data are expressed as medians rather
than frequency distributions.

Not surprisingly, Kurtz's (1973) dollar RCAs in San Ysidro
show lower fund shares than my data. If a median contribution of

Figure 2.7. Comparison of Fund Shares in Peso and Dollar
Informal and Intermediate RCAs

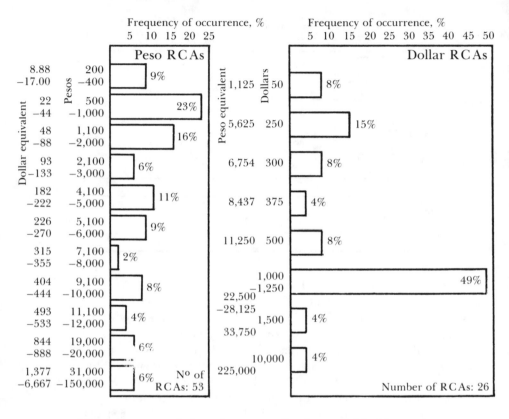

$7.50 is assumed (based on contributions of $5–10), and a membership of 10, then it is likely that the median fund share for the
San Ysidro RCAs is $75. My data show a much greater range
($50–10,000) with greatest frequency for fund shares between
$1,000 and $1,250 (representing 49% of associations), considerably above the San Ysidro median. Furthermore, 69 percent of
the RCAs involved contributions between $50 and $100 (see
Figure 3.3). Inflation by itself cannot account for these differences: in the period 1962–1964, the restaurant workers in the
Beverly Hills Hotel who made $150 a month had 5-person fund
shares of $350. The contrasts between Kurtz's data and these can
only be understood in relation to class differences.

The formal *mutualistas* of Mutualista de Yucatán had minimum fund shares of 10,000 pesos in 1978 (discontinued in 1979). Shares ranged from 10,000 to 150,000 pesos, with the distribution shown as in Table 2.1. Corporate officials were unwilling to divulge the frequency of each fund share.

The amounts involved in the VW or Datsun RCAs depended on the price of the automobile. At the time of my research these cars were estimated at 88,000 pesos excluding interest payments. It is highly probable that no VW or Datsun RCA is larger than 40 or 42 persons with the contribution between 2,000 and 2,200 pesos per month.

Length of Rotation Cycle

The length of the rotation cycle refers to the actual time it takes to complete all the turns in an RCA. As will be seen, there are congruent relationships between the number of participants, the amount contributed, the size of the fund share, and the length of the rotational cycle. For example, a 10-person RCA will usually disburse its funds on 10 evenly spaced occasions, whether weeks, months, or even years. The contributions will usually be in even amounts like $10 or 100 pesos. The amounts, however, may be split up so that participants may contribute $100 monthly in four weekly payments of $25. This practice, incidentally, does not necessarily occur among participants with limited incomes since in fact one of the most affluent RCAs, with $1,000 contributions used this method of payment. Nor is it necessarily the case, as the ethnographic literature has suggested, that the poorer the membership, the longer the cycle and the more spaced-out the payments (Embree 1939; Fei 1939; Fei and Chang 1948; Geertz 1962; Kurtz 1973). The shortest RCA was among transient laborers in Yucatán in which five buddies (*cuates*) made contributions of $8 a week (to be used for binges). I have already mentioned the longest continuing rotational cycle, which had lasted for 15 years when this research was being done. Its participants were middle management bank employees whose wives administered the process. This RCA was basically a hidden practice not acceptable to senior bank managers. The second longest cycle of 5 years was also found in a banking institution, with wives again administering the process.

These 5-week and 15-year rotation cycles represent the ex-
tremes. A 10–12 month cycle was most frequently found among
the informally organized RCA (see Figure 2.8) with a 2.5- to 3.5-
month rotational cycle next most frequent, and a 5.0- to 7.5-month
cycle the next.

The fact that the 10- to 12-month cycle is the most frequent,
however, points to the congruence between it and the popular
10- and 12-person RCAs (see Figure 2.1). A 10–12-month rotation cycle would be less likely to be congruent with a larger membership. In addition, however, the RCAs with fund shares of
$1,000–$1,250, which account for 49 percent of those shown in
Figure 2.6, are also congruent with 10–12 members in a 10–12-
month rotational cycle. Contributions of $50–100 occur most
often: almost 70 percent of the associations (35% + 4% + 30%;
see Figure 2.4) involved contributions in this range, and these
of course are the sums needed to make up the preferred fund
share of $1,000–1,250. It is likely that the rotation period of the
RCA, the number of members involved, and size of the fund
share are congruent. Ten persons contributing $100 a month for
10 months exactly make up the needed members for a $1,000
RCA. Twelve persons contributing the same amount for the same
period would account for a $1,200 RCA. Congruence and sym-

Figure 2.8. Rotation Cycles for Informal and Intermediate RCAs

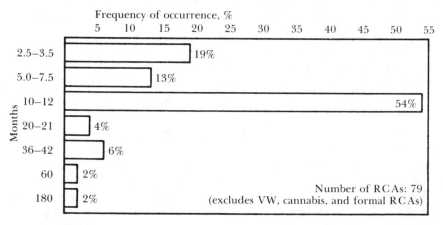

Note: The RCA of five weeks' duration referred to in the text is not included
in this tally.

metry seem to be selected for and provide RCA members a cultural artifact by means of which a predictive cycle of events and actions is usually kept in balance.

A similar relationship exists for the peso RCAs, with 49 percent of the associations involving contributions between 100 and 300 pesos, made up of between 10 and 12 persons, with fund shares between 1,000 and 3,000 pesos. Of the 53 peso RCAs analyzed only 4 were of the 500-peso variety, and 19 were between 1,000 and 3,000 pesos. This suggests that 36 percent (19 ÷ 53) of all peso RCAs were more than likely congruent with the modal characteristics of 10–12 persons, a fund share of 1,000–3,000 pesos, and a rotation of 10–12 months (10 persons × 100 pesos per month = 1,000 pesos). Other symmetrical permutations also result with contributed sums of 200–300 pesos, each of which will more than likely rotate in 10–12 months with a worth of 2,000–3,000 pesos.

In the formal *mutualistas* of Yucatán the rotational periods of course coincide exactly with the sums contributed and the number of persons participating in each *mutualista* (allowing for interest and fees). These relationships are carefully set down in tables which are followed by all participants.

For informal, intermediate, and formal RCAs, then, there is a strain toward symmetry of operation and participation, which acts as an important counterbalance to opposite pressures in urban living. Meaning is extracted from balancing factors even in commercialized RCAs. In other words, RCAs "make sense" as symmetrical expressions of the *confianza* construct, which itself is a symmetrical mechanism of balance. Such strain toward consistency and balance is also expressed in the way in which people refer to the RCAs, as the next section illustrates.

Commercial and Noncommercial RCAs

The literature on Mexican RCAs does not report examples of the organizer charging interest or other fees (Kurtz and Showman 1978; Lewis 1961, 1968; Lomnitz 1977), except for an undeveloped finding for *cundinas* (Kurtz 1973). Except for taking the first turn, no other reward has been suggested. However, this research has found widespread commercialized practices in which both a first turn and a "zero turn" (also referred to as "taking the zero") are taken by the organizer as a fee. Sometimes the first turn is the zero turn so that the organizer takes number 1 and does not make any contributions. In other words, the first turn may be a free first turn without any obligation on the part of the organizer to contribute anything to the RCA, and that free first turn is his or her compensation for organizing and administering the RCA. It is clear from the literature (Kurtz 1973; Kurtz and Showman 1978) that the taking of fees by specialists has not been considered analytically important to the definition of an informal RCA as commercialized. The opposite view prevails here.

In Mérida, commercial associations other than the corporate *mutualistas* also exist. These informal *mutualistas* consist of 40 or more members who contribute 88 pesos weekly for 40 weeks. Each member receives 3,200 pesos but pays 3,520 pesos. Thus the organizer makes a profit of 320 pesos per week for a total of 12,800 pesos. Theoretically, the larger the *mutualista*, the greater the risk of default, although default seldom occurs. In both large and small commercial RCAs there are several examples of full-time specialists who dedicate themselves totally to organizing residential and institutional RCAs.

As further illustration, consider an actual *cundina* in Tijuana in which 10 persons contributed $25 weekly, which was sorted out monthly. There were 11 actual monthly payments of $100 (4 × $25) by each of the 10 persons for a total of $1,000 monthly. The first turn or *el cero* of $1,000 went to the organizer, and the rest was sorted out to the participants over the following 10 months. When the organizer is also a participant, he or she receives a fee of $900 (not counting his or her contribution) but will also be among those rotating $900 (again excluding the organizer's contribution) during the life of the 10-member, 10-month *cundina*. In this particular *cundina* in Tijuana, the organizer was a full-time specialist who administered three RCAs simultaneously. Thus, analytically, fees charged by specialists structurally shift the exchange relations from generalized reciprocity to commercialized market exchange.

Some RCAs allow members to borrow on the not-yet-allocated share for a nominal fee. The organizer lends the money so that in the case cited above, a person could borrow $500 against the share of $900 and when the rotation was due, only receive $350. A discount of 10 percent is extracted by the organizer for the advance: $500 × 10 = $50, $50 subtracted from $400 = $350.

A majority of the informal and intermediate dollar and peso RCAs did not have a free first turn or fee. Of 66 dollar and peso RCAs, including RCAs without organizers, 58% (38) totally lacked any fees, free first turns, or zero turns. (Within such RCAs the first number could have been given to the organizer as recompense for his or her administrative work. The organizer would then continue to contribute to the RCA like the other participants.) On the other hand, in 6 percent (17) of the 66 RCAs, the organizers took the free first turn, *el cero*, and 17 percent (11) charged a 10 percent fee, or some other kind of charge, such as requiring more contributions than what was paid out. Forty-two percent of the RCAs in this research were commercialized to some extent.

Where the term *tanda* is used, those RCAs in which charges occur are called *tandas muertas* (dead RCAs) and those in which no money is made by an organizer, *tandas vivas*. The designation *tandas muertas* derives from the fact that the market relationship has replaced the normal reciprocally based relationship of the *tandas vivas*. As one organizer in the state of Veracruz put it, "They [*tandas muertas*] are nothing but business and so therefore I do not participate in them. They are not convivial. For me it is more important that they [the members] feel in *confianza* because this [RCA] is not a business. I have a business." On the other hand, another organizer for whom the RCAs are a business, rationalized the organization of *tandas muertas* in the following manner: "Life is not a gift so neither are my efforts."

This contrast between dead associations and live associations illustrates the profound social meanings attached to each. The *tanda viva* is alive because of the reciprocal expectations involved in social obligation based on mutual trust (*confianza*), and the phrase describing the dead RCAs as those in which the members are not convivial reflects the opposite of the living social fabric of the live RCAs. The *tanda muerta* is dead because the social obligation based on *confianza* is also dead and in its place is a material obligation for a service done by the organizer. Two modes of exchange, reciprocity and market exchange, are expressed even though the medium of exchange, money, is the same in both.

Such differentiation is made apparent and certain for participants by the congruence between such meaning and the symmetry of the RCA itself. That is, a *tanda viva* is alive because it balances equitably all the effort, trust, relationships, emotion, sacrifice, investment, and hard-earned money that make up the individual contributions. The medium of exchange is the certain and tangible proof of all these elements that go into making up a symmetrical social universe. The *tanda muerta*, on the other hand, is unbalanced, asymmetrical, and in the final analysis indeterminate—out of the individual participant's control. Not only is the *tanda* controlled only by the organizer, but fellowship, which is the basis of determinacy, is also dead.

USES OF FUNDS: SAVING TO SAVE

"It is really a wonderful savings—really" (*Es un ahorro bien bonito—de veras*), the informant said in the middle of a marketplace in the state of Chiapas. She captured what many RCA participants consider the primary use for the money accumulated in RCAs. Among 50 informants in Mexico and the United States who responded to an open-ended question on the manner in which these funds were used, the modal response (24%) was that they were used as savings. In fact, as has been previously mentioned, many persons, once they had saved enough to feel comfortable in institutions like banks or credit cooperatives, placed their funds in savings institutions. The second most frequent use, making up 17 percent of the responses, was that of fulfilling ritual obligations connected with Christmas, marriage, baptism, birthdays, saints' days, and anniversaries. Spending funds on household goods was the third most frequent response at 8 percent, while purchasing land, investing in income-producing activities, and paying debts each made up 7 percent of the responses. Buying clothes for children, using the money for vacations, and spending on unexpected problems, each constituted 5 percent of the responses. Figure 2.9 shows these frequencies.

As Kurtz and Showman (1978) have also stated, the single most important reason for participating in RCAs is to save money. It is important to note, however, that savings here are not simply determined by market relations. The quality of forced savings is important, since for many of our informants it is difficult to save in banking institutions. As further evidence will show, a person is obligated to save as part of multiple-stranded relations of friend-

Figure 2.9. Uses of RCA Funds

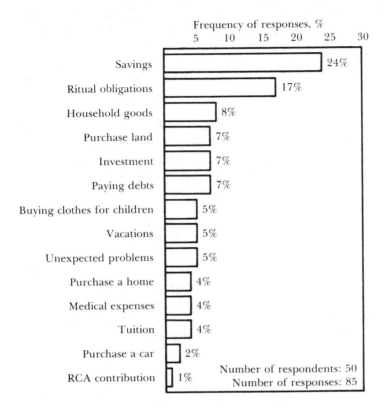

Frequency of responses, %

5	10	15	20	25	30

Savings — 24%
Ritual obligations — 17%
Household goods — 8%
Purchase land — 7%
Investment — 7%
Paying debts — 7%
Buying clothes for children — 5%
Vacations — 5%
Unexpected problems — 5%
Purchase a home — 4%
Medical expenses — 4%
Tuition — 4%
Purchase a car — 2%
RCA contribution — 1%

Number of respondents: 50
Number of responses: 85

ship, occupation, and kinship. Saving anchors the individual se-
curely within the networks of relations of which he or she is a
part, for it frees people to engage in social intercourse without
the disruption that would result from having to ask for the "favor"
of a loan to meet other obligations. Instead of affection turning to
instrumentation (Wolf 1956), savings generated by RCAs allow
social relations based on other sorts of obligations to be maintained. Saving in fact saves the multiplicity of relations from turning to singularity of interest.

Especially for those in *tandas vivas*, the saving of money takes
place within a dense social context, as does the spending of money
for ritual obligations. In this sense one becomes not only obligated
to give and to receive, but equally important, obligated to save.

Saving thus becomes a learning process, which expands when re-warded; a person not only learns to save money, but the obliga-tion to save becomes a positive reinforcing construct which con-tributes to the well-being of the multiplicity of dense relations that make up a symmetrical social universe.

The use of these funds, it should be remembered, has class-specific dimensions. To recapitulate, saving and ritual obligations are important in working-class and marginal sectors, but other sectors use their money to escape the stresses of overindebtedness. Within middle-class sectors, RCA participation is one of the chief methods used to maintain an expected standard of living. On the other hand, there are networks of professionals for whom the fund share is relatively unimportant and who spend it on what-ever they please. Not only do the characteristics of the RCAs themselves vary in relation to class sectors, but so do the uses of the funds.

Modes of productive activity can also influence the use of RCA funds. In Los Angeles, for example, clothing workers who had worked at piece rates frequently used accumulated *cundinas* to open their own sweatshops. In Ciudad Netzahualcoyótl, petty merchants used *tandas* to invest in merchandise which they sold at a substantial profit. Thus RCAs can also serve as steps in vertical mobility, especially among petty entrepreneurs.

3 Social and Cultural Contexts and Implications

CONTEXTS AND SECTORS

The seriousness with which RCAs are regarded among many social sectors can be simply illustrated by the following ledger of payments due immediate attention. The ledger belonged to an individual in Chapala, a lakeside town an hour's drive from Guadalajara (the translation is mine):

Pagos (payments)
1. Pago de deuda (debt payment)
2. tanda—200 pesos
3. uniformes de niños (children's uniforms)
4. compra de mercancía (purchase of merchandise)
5. Pedro (Peter—no explanation)
6. pago de muebles (furniture payment)
7. mercancía (merchandise)
8. bautizo (baptism)
9. coperativa (cooperative)
10. personal (personal)

There, second on his list of debts, stands this individual's RCA obligation. There is no need to speculate as to whether the ranking reflects their actual importance or whether money was actually dispensed to meet these obligations. It is enough to note that for this individual the RCA obligation came to mind right after his debt payment and before his children's uniforms.

The popularity of the RCA can be appreciated by observing the myriad contexts and social sectors in which it appears. While reference to class sectors has been made in previous sections of this work, and a variety of different types of operations has been discussed, the following analysis lists in detail most of the contexts and sectors in which RCAs have been found, both in this research and in that reported by others. Those already discussed will be dealt with in less detail in this section. I also categorize RCAs according to the contexts in which they were found, identify the class sector to which they probably belong, and discuss the importance of the social and cultural permutations that appear for each category and class sector.

RCAs were found in all class sectors in Mexico except the highest echelons of private and public executive domains, such as industrialists and members of the international academic elite. Their familial networks probably do not participate in RCAs. Whereas RCAs touch most class sectors and occupational niches in Mexico, those found in the southwestern United States basically include only working-class and marginal sectors. One was reported to exist among professionals, including the company officers of a southwestern food producer's corporation, in Los Angeles. I have been unable to verify its existence.

Three categories of RCAs were developed: residential RCAs of all class sectors, occupational RCAs, and for lack of a better term, "familial" RCAs. The last term refers to RCAs made up of people who are primarily related to each other by kinship or friendship rather than by residence or occupation. None of the three categories, however, should be thought of as exclusive. Since membership is relatively fluid in some RCAs, and in fact residential, occupational, and familial RCAs all include aspects of the others, the three categories should be thought of as analytical constructs.

Residence

Residential RCAs were found in Mexico in all of the sites studied. In Monterrey, for example, three residential RCAs represented three class sectors: one was located in a marginal economic residential sector occupied by squatters (*paracaidistas*, literally "parachutists"), another in a largely working-class area of blue- and white-collar workers, and the third in a middle-class residential area of largely professional or highly skilled industrial and government technicians. In each class sector, for the most part, the RCAs were controlled by women who were both organizers and participants. In the squatter area, for example, contributions to the *tandas* were siphoned from spouses' allowances for household expenses. In the squatter area, and in most squatter settlements, the usual fund share is between 400 and 500 pesos with a contribution of 20–50 pesos weekly, depending on the number of shares in the *tanda*. However, *tandas* do exist with contributions of 10 pesos and fund shares of 20 pesos. From a woman's monthly allowance of 200 pesos, 10–25 pesos will be saved weekly for RCA contributions. For the most part, in Monterrey these *tandas* involved relatively small contributions and fund shares, and were made up of persons who were well known by all the residents or recommended by someone of mutual trust within the older links of the RCA networks.

In the working-class district, higher contributions and fund shares reflected the higher incomes. From their husband's allowance these women generally saved a proportionally larger amount than the economically marginal women, but they still relied on the same cultural construct of *confianza* as the stabilizing glue within the RCAs. The middle-class residential *tandas* seemed to be larger. The members shared some recreational interest, such as playing cards. They referred to their RCAs as part of their club activities, coterminous with playing canasta or some other card game and the exchange of gifts. With approximately 40 women in each club contributing 1,000 pesos monthly, the residential middle-class RCAs in Monterrey rotated substantial amounts.

This notion of a club which was quite common among middle-class residential sectors, was extended to upper-class sectors in other areas. I have already mentioned the women in the Lomas de Chapultepec who combined gift giving with contributing large amounts for "sumptuous consumption." These women generally referred to their activities in terms of a residential club and in fact elected officers who presided over various club affairs. For these women, who receive an allowance from their husbands of 20,000 pesos monthly, the Monterrey women's *tandas* of 1,000 pesos deal in paltry sums. In addition, in Tapachula and Tijuana, this same club phenomenon was exhibited in combination with recreational, gift-giving, and very importantly, commensal activities.

This middle- and upper-class phenomenon of integrating the RCA into clubs and combining it with elaborate commensal activities and with other recreational activities is in clear contrast to the pattern seen in marginal and working-class RCAs. The latter for the most part were 10-person RCAs composed of neighbors who were also friends and in many cases also kinswomen. These women did not have the time, the resources, or the inclination to meet regularly as part of their ordinary activities. The recreational aspect was taken care of for these women individually if the organizer delivered the fund share personally, and on the one occasion when all the women got together and selected the numbers of the *tandas* in a drawing. For these women, recreational activities were organized along "natural systems" of relationships based on residence and kinship. For the middle- and upper-class women, recreational activities consisted of cultural events deliberately organized usually on the basis of residence alone.

Regardless of whether a residential RCA was of the club or the natural system type, in at least 50 percent of the cases, the free first turn, zero turn, or a fee was taken by the organizer. This was not done in Lomas de Chapultepec or the upper-middle-class "clubs" in Tijuana, where such a fee would be considered *déclassé*. Among working-class residents of Tijuana, however, an organizer who charged fees presented each member with a registration card on which appeared the information shown in Figure 3.1.

The registration card shows that in this residential RCA, there were 10 numbers, and Sra. Concha whose name appears at the upper left-hand corner was number 6. Under the first column appear the numbers 1–10 with four check marks to the right of each number except 6. The check marks refer to four payments made for that particular number. Next to number 6 appears the signature of the organizer. That signature indicates that the organizer gave the fund share to the member whose countersignature appears on the same line in the third column. The middle column refers to the date on which the final payment was made for that number. The column under *cantidad* (amount) refers to the four installments made weekly for the monthly contribution of 480 pesos. In this case, the fee for the organizer was included in each installment. Thus for each 120-peso installment, 20 pesos went to the organizer, so that monthly he or she received 80 pesos from each person. Since the person receiving the turn does not pay for that month, the organizer receives 720 pesos per month from the nine other persons who do make their contributions. The organizer in these residential RCAs will have earned at the end of the RCA a total of 7,200 pesos (720 × 10 turns), and each member will have paid 4,320 pesos and received 3,600 pesos.

Even though under the fee or zero-turn residential RCA there is a net loss for the participant, this form of savings is still preferred by many working-class and marginal-sector women, and not

Figure 3.1. Registration Card

Sra. Concha nombre (name)								
numero (number) 6			fecha (date)	cantidad (amount)				
1. √ √ √ √				6 de Marzo	120	120	120	120
2. √ √ √ √				2 de Abril	120	120	120	120
3. √ √ √ √				2 de Mayo	120	120	120	120
4. √ √ √ √				8 de Juño	120	120	120	120
5. √ √ √ √				9 de Julio	120	120	120	120
6. Almendra López				10 de Agosto	Sra Concha V.			
7. √ √ √ √				10 de Septiembre	120	120	120	120
8. √ √ √ √				6 de Octubre	120	120	120	120
9. √ √ √ √				6 de Noviembre	120	120	120	120
10. √ √ √ √				7 de Diciembre	120	120	120	120

because they lack "economic" motivation or insight. Many women for psychological reasons prefer to save what they can in an RCA rather than earn interest from a commercial institution. They prefer to "maximize" the certainty of what seems to be the organizer's personal interest rather than the uncertainty of an institution's impersonal interest.

Among residential RCAs in which no direct economic advantage is provided to the organizer, two other sorts of advantages exist. The first occurs in nonfee RCAs organized by petty merchants who live in the area in which they sell. In marginal and working-class sectors, these organizers recruit potential members from women who live in their commercial territories. In such cases an organizer's visit could be for the purpose of collecting the contributions of the RCA member, delivering the fund share, or collecting money owed for merchandise. Yet because these women are under a double obligation—for the RCA, one based on reciprocity; for the purchased merchandise, one based on the market exchange relationship—they do not hide from the salesperson-organizer. The second advantage accrues to store owners whose customers belong to store RCAs. In these there is no charge, nor is the zero taken by the store owner, but most customers who are RCA members also have a charge account with the store. This was especially true of pharmacies.

In other residential RCAs no such advantages were found. Instead, the RCAs with few kinship members or occupational cohorts were organized around some other element, such as a neighborhood political party center, a prestigious member of the residential sector such as an older woman known for providing advice, or a local political leader with intense social networks made up of women.

Among some middle-class and professional sectors different advantages accrued to the organizer. In a border region, one woman who organized separate associations among women and men from the same social milieu did not charge the women who belonged to her RCAs and clubs. She was a member of an intimate social network of women who participated in the same recreational and commensal activities, who visited each other's homes, and whose children attended the same private schools. Their husbands were generally in the same voluntary associations and professional sectors, if not occupations, and participated in the same set of community political activities. In the RCAs she organized among the husbands, she took the zero turn. Because she participated and held leadership positions in the same community political activities and voluntary associations as the husbands, she was considered to be an insider in the men's organizational activities, but not part of the old boy networks. She was enough of an insider to establish market relations with the men and charge a fee for her RCA services, but not enough of one to establish reciprocal obligations and relationships. On the other hand, the *confianza* she enjoyed with their wives was established within the intimacy required of wives and women. She parlayed the advantages of both insider and outsider to make a substantial amount of money.

In both fee and nonfee residential RCAs with a substantial

membership, rotation of commensal activities and fund shares usually occurred at each turn, except in the most marginal economic sectors. In RCAs with more than 20 women members, fund shares were likely to be allotted by a drawing. Each drawing would be attended by the women who had not yet received their turn. Thus for at least the first 10 weeks (of a weekly 35-person RCA), about half of the women whose turn had not yet been allotted would show up for a drawing for the following week's share at the home of the person whose turn had been selected the previous week. By the eighteenth week the number present at the drawings would be considerably reduced. By the thirtieth week it was not unusual for the last 5 to have their names drawn at one time and have their fund share distributed together in a preselected home. At each drawing the hostess was expected to provide some refreshments such as soft drinks or cake so that such occasions generated information exchanges. The point is that regardless of whether or not fees are charged in RCAs, generalized reciprocal exchange is generated during such events.

In the southwestern United States, there is little variation among residential RCAs except for the fact that I have not found them in upper-middle-class residential areas. There are, however, few upper-middle-class areas in the United States predominantly inhabited by Mexicans. Except in working-class or economically marginal Mexican *barrios* (neighborhoods) such as those in East Los Angeles, portions of San Pedro, Monterey Park, and Wilmington, residential RCAs are not as common as in Mexico. In most of those analyzed the organizer had established long-standing *confianza* relationships with the members through occupation, kinship, or residence. These were not purely residential RCAs, in fact, and unlike most RCAs in Mexico, included both men and women, with women tending to predominate.

Even with *confianza*, some residential fixity, and kinship affiliation, many of these RCAs, unlike most of those in Mexico, collected their weekly contributions and delivered the fund share at the same time. Such is the residential mobility among wage earners, that residential fixity is difficult to maintain for extended periods, especially in the Los Angeles area. The shift to zero- or free-first-turn-based RCAs is a phenomenon congruent with such mobility, and one may speculate that commercialized practices appeared originally because organizers cannot establish *confianza* in a mobile population, not because they "learn" profit motives. The latter is not excluded from consideration, but an organizer's switch from a nonfee to a fee RCA may have its genesis in disrupted social relations rather than economic motives. This may also be the case in Mexico, especially in areas of rapid population shifts like the border cities and central Mexico.

Such mobility, for example, can be noted in the origins of the membership of one originally noncommercialized residential *cundina* in Hollywood. The organizer was from the Mexican state of Sinaloa while her huband, who also participated in the RCA, was from the state of Durango. Two other male members were brothers-in-law from the city of Guadalajara. One woman came from Guatemala, two sisters had just arrived from Mazatlán in Sinaloa, and the last member was a woman from the state of Michoacán. Equally important, however, is the fact that all were renters of apartments or small homes and stayed an average of 2.3 years each per rental. All had been in the United States for 10 to 20 years, including visits to Mexico of less than 1 year's duration. For these persons, inflationary rent increases, wage-sector changes, and voluntary and involuntary returns to their country of origin had caused frequent residential shifts. For organizers such conditions and pressures create uncertainty and force them to take out the "insurance" of a first free turn or zero.

The residential diversity apparent in the informal rotating credit association can be represented by categorizing residential areas according to the approximate occupational level of their inhabitants. High white collar includes professional occupations and proprietors; low white collar, semiprofessional and service-oriented occupations and small business proprietors; high blue collar, skilled industrial and crafts jobs; low blue collar, semi-skilled and unskilled occupations; finally, "other" includes students, welfare recipients, prisoners, the unemployed, and the retired. Table 3.1 shows the social diversity of residential areas in 80 informal rotating credit associations in Mexico and the United States (intermediate and formal ones are excluded). Also included are areas reported by Cope and Kurtz (1980), Kurtz (1973), Kurtz and Showman (1978), Lewis (1959, 1961, 1968), and Lomnitz (1977).

It is not suggested that the various residential areas and class

Table 3.1. Social Diversity by Occupational Structure
in Informal Rotating Credit Associations (N = 80)

Area	City	Occupational Structure:				
		HWC	LWC	HBC	LBC	Other
Northern Mexico	Monterrey, Nuevo León	+	+	+	+	+
Northern Mexico	Mexicali, Tijuana,[1] and Ensenada, Baja California	+	+	+	+	+
Northern Mexico	Ciudad Juárez, Chihuahua	−	+	+	+	+
Northern Mexico	Chihuahua, Chihuahua	−	+	+	+	+
Northern Mexico	Concordia, Mazatlán, and Culiacán, Sinaloa	−	+	+	+	+
Central Mexico	Mexico City,[2] Federal District, Ciudad Netzahualcoyótl, state of Mexico	+	+	+	+	+
Central Mexico	Guanajuato, Guanajuato	−	+	+	+	+
Central Mexico	Puebla,[3] San Felipe, and San Jerónimo, Puebla	−	+	+	+	+
South-central Mexico	Guadalajara, Chapala, and Tonalá Jalisco	+	+	+	+	+
Southern Mexico (Gulf side)	Mérida, Yucatán	+	+	+	+	+
Southern Mexico (Gulf side)	Poza Rica, Papantla, and Jalapa, Veracruz	+	+	+	+	+
Southern Mexico (Guatemala side)	Tapachula, San Cristóbal de las Casas, and Tuxtla Gutiérrez, Chiapas	+	+	+	+	+
Southern Mexico (Guatemala side)	Oaxaca, Oaxaca	−	+	+	+	+
Southwestern United States	El Paso, Texas	−	+	+	+	+

Table 3.1. Social Diversity by Occupational Structure
in Informal Rotating Credit Associations (N = 80)

Area	City	Occupational Structure:				
		HWC	LWC	HBC	LBC	Other
Southwestern United States	San Diego, San Ysidro,[1] Chula Vista, and National City, California	−	+	+	+	+
Southwestern United States	Los Angeles,[5] San Pedro, Wilmington, Hollywood, and Beverly Hills, California	−	+	+	+	+
Southwestern United States	Unincorporated East Los Angeles	−	+	+	+	+

Source: Vélez-Ibañez 1982.
Note: HWC = high white collar, LWC = low white collar, HBC = high blue collar, LBC = low blue collar, Other = students, welfare recipients, retired persons, prisoners, and unemployed workers.
    1. Reported by Kurtz (1973) and verified by this research.
    2. Reported by Lewis (1959, 1961, 1968) and Lomnitz (1977) and verified by this research.
    3. Reported by Kurtz and Showman (1978) and Cope and Kurtz (1980).
    4. Reported by Kurtz (1973) and verified by this research.
    5. Includes West Los Angeles.

sectors are representative in a statistical sense of the distribution of such sectors within the 80 informal rotating credit associations studied. However, the sectors and areas in which the associations are found are representative of the social structure of Mexico and of the ethnic and social structure of Mexicans in the United States.

As Table 3.1 illustrates, in Mexico all social sectors are represented, but further empirical study is needed to verify whether rotating associations are present or not in HWC residential areas in Ciudad Juárez, Chihuahua, Culiacán, Guanajuato, Puebla, and Oaxaca. It is unlikely that any HWC residential RCAs will be found in the southwestern United States since, as I have pointed out, most Mexicans in such sectors are dispersed in nonethnic residential areas.

Occupation

Probably the best source of contextual data in both Mexico and the southwestern United States is occupational sectors. The usual occupational RCAs are of two types: those in which the employees of a firm are both participants and organizers, and those composed of employees but organized by nonemployees. The former are the most noncommercial of the informal RCAs, except for familial RCAs.

Mexican film theater chains in Los Angeles have both types of occupational RCAs, and it is well to consider these in some detail in order to appreciate both their differences and their similarities. This discussion also provides insights into the structural contexts in which membership in such associations occurs.

Within employee-organized RCAs in Mexican theater chains in Los Angeles, two subtypes appear which are also found in other businesses: those in which the manager is the organizer and those in which employees who are at the same level do the organizing. In the former, the RCA participants may ask the manager to be an impartial money keeper using the local theater's accounting system, or the manager may initiate an RCA in order to make a profit from a free first turn or zero. When the manager does not also participate there is a tendency for the employee-initiated RCA to shift to a more intermediate sort. However, the manager usually hides the RCA from the chain's general management. Since the organizer is always a cultural group member, RCAs in theaters having non-Hispanic managers do not shift to intermediate RCAs.[1] Those managers who have been asked to be money holders or accountants tend to be perceived as organizers in later RCAs, and, in time, the practice becomes integrated into the normal operating activities of the theater. Such a process, however, can be interrupted if a new manager is appointed.

The RCAs initiated by the manager begin as intermediate practices with bookkeeping procedures. More than half of a single theater's employees are likely to participate. In employee-initiated RCAs, fewer employees within any one theater participate, but the membership includes employees from other theaters.

In RCAs in which same-level employees are organizers and

participants, the associations are organized by the cashiers rather than the ticket takers, candy and refreshment vendors, ushers, or janitorial employees.[2] The reasons seem to derive from the cashiers' obvious facility with numbers, which provides them with some legitimacy. The cashiers, all of whom are women, have ready access to informational networks encompassing all the theaters within the various chains. Since they are literally out front, they are highly visible as representatives of the particular theater and therefore have public reputations of trust. Their reputations are in fact nurtured through the telephone. In every cashier's booth is a telephone used to answer questions about performance sched-ules and the like. The cashiers, however, also use the telephone to organize employee-directed RCAs and keep each other in-formed about who is ill on the days contributions are collected, whose turn has been reached, who has informed them of late pay-ments, and the latest information on anyone who is likely to leave his or her job. This is extremely important since those who leave are less likely to contribute to the fund.

While the RCAs indigenous to the theaters have a reciprocal quality which is reflected in the seriousness with which employees invest money, energy, and trust in such associations, the same can-not be said of the more commercialized RCAs organized by out-siders. In these, there is more conflict over payments and more local-level political competition. Both organizers and participants agreed that "everyone faithfully receives the fund share but is very hesitant to pay the contribution." On the other hand, both agreed that "like all Mexicans, we are honorable." This aspect of receiving but hesitating to fulfill an obligation, but by obligation carrying out that obligation, marks the basic relationship between theater employees and outside organizers. This is because such organizers are not part of the natural systems of close interper-sonal networks of the theater employees. The employees are ob-liged to interact socially with the outside organizer as though they were part of a noncommercialized employee RCA. Yet the instru-mental interest of the organizer is resented, and ambivalent rela-tionships between them ensue.

This ambivalence is expressed, for example, during the collec-tion period in which the *cundinero* (someone who collects money commercially) seeks out the employees for their contributions. Collections are made during rest and eating periods, and for the most part, the *cundinero* is met by derisive remarks and hooting. As the organizer approaches a group of employees, it is not uncommon to hear barely audible remarks like "*Tiene cara de ladrón*" (He has the face of a thief) or "*No más quiere para pagar sus borracheras*" (He only wants money for his drunken binges). Worse, however, among Mexican men is the overheard remark: "*No mas quiere para su mujer y así nos obliga*" (He only wants money for his woman and that is why he obligates us). The underlying meaning is that the organizer is supposedly under the control of a woman and indirectly obligates the members of the RCA to be under her control since they contribute to her support through the organizer's RCA.

Other *flechazos* (barbs) said to the organizer's face upon his arrival included "*Ya le cayó vidrio al agua*" (Glass has fallen on still waters, or Still waters have turned to glass which breaks). Equally direct was the sentence "*Ya tan bien que estábamos y la veniste a fregar*" (We were so comfortable and now you have come to spoil it). More direct, as he was sitting down with the employees, were personal labels such as *cabrón* (cuckold), *ratero* (racketeer), and *estafador* (cheater). Yet none of the overheard remarks, direct barbs, or personal labels could be uttered if in fact *confianza* had not been established. In working-class sectors personal insult is not taken lightly, and both verbal and physical responses should be expected. Therefore even though the organizer is considered an enemy, he is also a friend, and thus the joking expresses the inherent contradictions between the instrumentality and affectivity of those roles.

Problems, however, do arise with manager-controlled intermediate RCAs in some of the other business contexts. There have been reports that in some restaurant RCAs in which the owners are also the organizers, the owner procrastinates about turning over the employees' fund share and threatens to dismiss any who voice complaints. In one chain of Mexican restaurants in central Los Angeles, the father-daughter owners consistently withhold pay from their employees for their *cundinas*, take the first free turn, but rotate the *cundina* share weeks late. They are able to do this because most of their employees are "undocumented workers" and have few legal recourses. In such cases where *confianza* is violated, employees quit. For the most part cheating by organizers is rare.

Cheating does not occur among the employee-organized *cundinas* in the theaters, in ceramic factories in West Los Angeles, and among garment workers in central Los Angeles, Chula Vista, and San Diego. In those contexts, the process of cultural and behavioral exclusion is quite marked so that only those with proven *confianza* are invited to join. As is discussed in the next section behavioral nuances are carefully noted, and persons not meeting quite explicit standards are frankly excluded from participation in spite of employment seniority and stable salaries.

In Mexico, a broader representation of occupational sectors was involved in the RCAs. In the professions, there were many RCAs among medical practitioners, especially in large clinics. Specific medical areas had their own status-specific RCAs. For example, in one medical clinic in Monterrey, the doctors had their own RCA of 20,000 pesos, the pharmacy employees another of 15,000 pesos, general medical assistants a third of 5,000 pesos, and the records and administrative personnel another of 1,500 pesos. Occasionally one of the pharmacy employees might engage in the doctor's RCA, but he would deal only with the interns and not with the staff physicians. Nurses would not only have their own RCA, but female nurses would also be quite free to engage in all of the other RCAs except those of staff doctors. It would seem that female nurses, simply because they are women, are exempted from the usual status restrictions.

In the National Social Security System (Seguro Social) throughout Mexico, and in city, state, and federal agencies, RCAs were quite well developed in most administrative and nonadministrative sectors. In the National Anthropology Museum in Mexico City, RCAs crosscut departmental divisions among working-class employees. Each department head (*maestro*) was in charge of an RCA in which employees from several departments participated. The museum is divided administratively into various sections, each responsible for maintaining artifacts of a particular material, such as plastics, leather, metal, wood, and cloth and thread. In addition, the clerical and administrative assistants were engaged in separate RCAs from those of the skilled technicians. At the time of this research no upper-level administrators or professional anthropological staff participated. Indeed, few of the professional staff were even aware of the existence of the RCAs in the museum or in the general literature.

Yet in most private and public bureaucracies RCAs were found. Among the administrative staff of PEMEX (Petroleros Enérgicos de Mexico) in Veracruz; the librarians of Mérida; the maintenance crews of the transit departments and their administrative heads in Monterrey; the tourist departments of Tijuana; the middle administrative level of the Central Bank of Mexico in Mexico City; the police department of Tapachula; the officers and directors of the International Brotherhood of Voluntary Associations (a pseudonym) of Mexicali; the maintenance workers at the University of Southern California and their cohorts in the National University in Mexico City (UNAM)—in all these groups the rotating credit association was well rooted.

Table 3.2 shows the actual occupations found within the 90

Table 3.2. Occupational Structure of Participants in Rotating Credit Associations
(N = 90)

Category	Occupation
High white collar Professional Proprietors	Executive managers, lawyers, physicians, businessmen/and women, architects, academics, bankers, upper-level bureaucrats, researchers, accountants, economists, psychiatrists
Low white collar Semiprofessional Small business Service (social)	Tellers, typists, stenographers, office workers, librarians, teachers, bartenders, traveling saleswomen and men, pharmacists, bookkeepers, cashiers, clerks, theater employees, produce market proprietors, nurses, social workers, tourist guides, food vendors, reporters, policemen
High blue collar Skilled (industrial) Craftsmen	Oil-field workers, technicians, electricians, welders, telephone employees, ceramicists, factory workers, projectionists, museum craftsmen, fishermen
Low blue collar Semiskilled Unskilled	Waiters and waitresses, busboys, assemblers, seamstresses, pottery shapers, janitors, maintenance workers, laborers, day laborers, street hawkers, domestics, guards, nightwatchmen, gardeners, taxi drivers, hotel busmen
Other	Students, welfare recipients, retired persons, prisoners, unemployed workers

Source: Vélez-Ibañez 1982.

rotating credit associations examined in this study. Because of the
many ambiguities and difficulties involved in classifying occupations, the participants' actual occupations are listed next to the
general occupational categories in Table 3.2.

As can be seen from Table 3.2, the occupations represented in
this study cover a wider range than those previously mentioned
in the literature. Cope and Kurtz (1980) report that participants
in the Puebla area are associated with industry, with the largest
number in the category of workers. Their occupational classifica-
tion differs from the one used here, but their data do not seem to
show any high-white-collar participants. My sample is not techni-
cally a random one, so it is not possible to claim that my categories
are representative in a statistical sense of the actual distribution
of occupations among rotating credit association members. What
can be said with certainty, however, is that the occupations reported here do represent the occupational structure of Mexicans
in their own country and in the United States.

Familial

Familial RCAs occur within marginal, working-class, and petty
bourgeois sectors. Kinship relationships are the embedded networks used as the foundation for RCAs. In addition, intimate
friends of the family who have no recognized familial relationships
other than intimacy also engage in these associations. Such relationships are dense and multiple and generate reciprocity without
the intervening market relations that mark the more commercialized RCAs.

By density I mean "the extent to which links which could possibly exist among persons do in fact exist" (Mitchell 1969: 18).
These links are potentially available to stimulate some kind of
exchange; such exchanges can involve emotions, resources, support, and also disapproval. These potential exchanges are in turn
closely related to the social relations that have been established in
recreational, residential, employment, kinship, religious, political,
and any other human domains. When the same people are engaged in a number of the same domains, then multiple (multiplex)
relations between them will have been generated. Thus in the
tanda illustrated in Figures 3.2–3.6, the organizer's best friend was
an important member, had the same surname, was from the same

Figure 3.2. Armando–Felipe

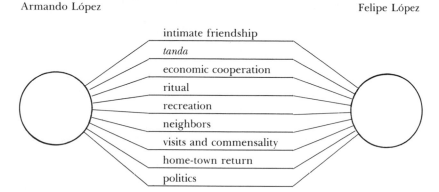

Armando López

Felipe López

intimate friendship

tanda

economic cooperation

ritual

recreation

neighbors

visits and commensality

home-town return

politics

Source: Vélez-Ibañez 1980.

town, engaged in the same business, lived in the same area, and had participated in the same political activities. They frequented the same bars and dance halls, visited each other's homes, and celebrated holidays together. Both returned to their home town to celebrate the fiestas for that town's patron saint and maintained and replicated equivalent sorts of relationships there. Both transported to sell at the fiestas merchandise that they had purchased jointly to increase their volume discount.

Figure 3.2 illustrates these multiple relations between the organizer, Armando López, and his intimate friend Felipe López (both names are pseudonyms). It must be pointed out that the relationships represented are partial and do not include those between Felipe and the rest of the *tanda* membership or among the other members. What is presented here to illustrate the density and multiplicity of relationships is only an example of the ego-centered networks of the organizer with those of his *tanda* network. In a later section, the entire network of another *tanda* is presented, showing in detail the interesting balance of such familial *tandas*.

The relationships between Armando and his younger brother Tomás López, a second member of the *tanda*, are illustrated in Figure 3.3. Tomás has a small tailor's shop a block from Armando's home. Tomás's eldest female child was baptized by Armando which ties the brothers as *compadres* (cogodparents), as well as

Figure 3.3. Armando–Tomás

Armando López   Tomás López

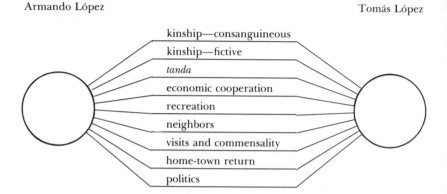

kinship—consanguineous

kinship—fictive

tanda

economic cooperation

recreation

neighbors

visits and commensality

home-town return

politics

making Armando *compadre* to his brother's wife. The brothers co-operate economically. Armando buys bolts of cloth at discounts through his business, and Tomás and his wife make inexpensive dresses for Armando to sell door-to-door to customers in Ciudad Netzahualcoyótl. Both men participated in the same political protests, and both participate in the ritual celebration of their home town saint's day as well. Almost nightly Armando and Tomás meet in Armando's grocery store to drink beer before going home.

The relationships of the third *tanda* member are complicated. Mrs. Guadalupe Luna is Tomás's mother-in-law, lives in a different neighborhood of the same city, engages in the same ritual and commensal activities as Armando for such important events as birthdays, saints' days, national holidays, and religious observances, and visits Armando's household with some frequency. The relationship is complicated by Tomás's heavy drinking. He overspends his limited income and borrows money from Mrs. Luna for household expenses. Mrs. Luna must call upon Armando for two basic reasons: first, to ask him to serve as a domestic broker between Tomás and her daughter when quarrels erupt over Tomás's drinking, and second, to collect money when Tomás does not pay back what he owes her. Armando on occasion has given Mrs. Luna's contribution to the *tanda* to pay debts incurred by his brother. On other occasions, Armando has paid Mrs. Luna money owed her by Tomás. Figure 3.4 shows the levels of multiplicity in this relationship within the *tanda*.

Figure 3.4. Armando–Mrs. Luna

Armando López   Mrs. Guadalupe Luna

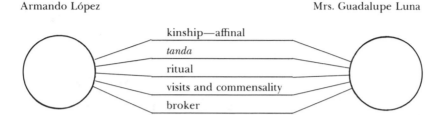

kinship—affinal

tanda

ritual

visits and commensality

broker

Graciela López, Armando and Tomás's oldest sister, is the fourth member of the *tanda*. Since she resides in the same household as Armando, keeps house for him, assists in his business, participates in all ritual and commensal activities, and returns to their home town with Armando, Graciela's relations with Armando are quite dense. As important, however, is the fact that Armando is Graciela's main source of support and the authority figure for her and her 10-year-old son, all of whom reside in a kind of primary group replication in the household. Figure 3.5 shows the complexity of their relationships.

The fifth and final member of the *tanda*, not including Armando, is Mrs. María Cicote, the next-door neighbor. She is also within Armando's kinship network, since her son married Armando's younger sister Virginia. Mrs. Cicote also has a small sewing business and purchases cloth from Armando, who sells on consignment the clothing she makes. She orders special sewing jobs from Tomás as well, but there is no competition between them since the articles they make are intended for entirely different functions. Mrs. Cicote and Armando share ritual and some commensal and recreational activities, and they visit daily to talk over business or family matters. Figure 3.6 shows these various relationships.

As the diagrams illustrate, the organizer has built his *tanda* operation on a variety of intimate familial relations. The diagrams do not, however, indicate the quality of those relationships, only the potential density and multiplicity of ties. Boissevain (1974) and Kapferer (1969) have tried to measure "transactional content," or the quality of multiple relations, by measuring the elements exchanged in each relation. While these attempts are

Figure 3.5. Armando–Graciela

Armando López   Graciela López

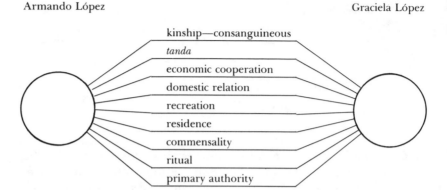

kinship—consanguineous
tanda
economic cooperation
domestic relation
recreation
residence
commensality
ritual
primary authority

laudatory and meaningful in social arenas beyond primary group activities, within the intimate networks described here such an analysis is not a fruitful exercise.

The values a culture places on nonmaterial and material exchange are relative and vary with the particular cultural system. While it is certainly methodologically possible to ascertain some hierarchy of value or values, comparing before and after states when individuals' contexts and fortunes are shifting would be very difficult. For Mexicans, *compadrazgo* (cogodparenthood) is a highly valued personal relation, especially between *cuates* (pals) like Armando and Felipe. But the relation between brother and sister is also extremely intimate. Within such intimate familial networks of *confianza*, the qualitative dimensions of exchange must be described culturally and not in terms of a numerically operationalized standard.

To understand the cultural dimension it is necessary to rely on the anthropologist's observational material and the best scaling techniques of cultural extraction available. Assuming this statement is correct, Armando's *tanda* can be understood best as one embedded in the most intimate of culturally valued networks, and contextually expressed by the constant reliance on reciprocal exchanges of symbols, artifacts, affect, assistance, favors, intimacies, commensality, ritual cooperation, and even money. The quality of these relations does not stem from the number of exchanges, but rather from the reciprocal exchange of culturally valued material and nonmaterial artifacts. It is probable that in such intimate

Figure 3.6. Armando–Mrs. Cicote

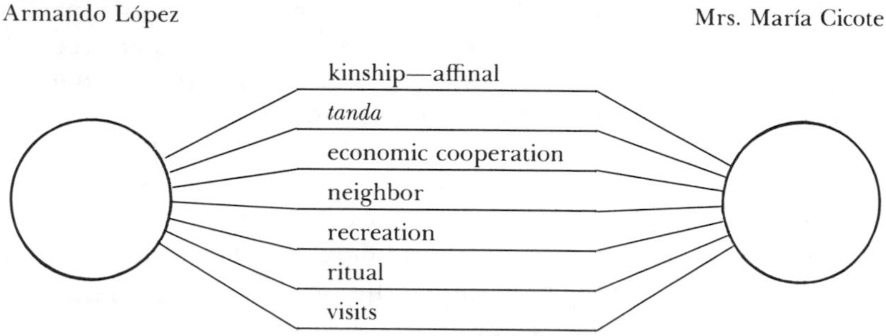

Armando López   Mrs. María Cicote

contexts more will be exchanged, but quantity does not affect the quality of the exchange. More may be exchanged, but if what is exchanged is not culturally valued and within the reciprocal mode, then the quality and density of the multiple relations are questionable.

Each context and sector analyzed here, such as residence, occupation, and family, has distributed within it various culturally constituted values which vary according to the quality of the relationships. However, the greater the congruence between the reciprocal exchange mode and those relationships, the more likely the occurrence of intensity and intimacy. Their presence can only be determined through observation and intimate knowledge of the cultural system of each context.

Underlying all the contexts discussed here is the cultural quality of fixity. Each context is culturally constituted, fixing persons in categories and relationships, which are used as physical, emotional, and social references. Yet each context, be it familial, occupational, or residential, is mutable and cannot supply permanent references or the means to fix persons permanently. Such is the paradox that unfolds from our data, but in this paradox lies the key to understanding the importance of such a practice as the rotating credit association.

RISKS AND SAFEGUARDS

In his excellent discussion of the ethnic rotating credit association in the United States,[3] Light (1972: 59) has stated that risk is an innate property of lending, and that risks exist even for those engaged in informally based RCAs like the familial ones described in this work. Light notes, however, that for members of Japanese and Chinese RCAs in the United States such risk is appreciably reduced because these RCAs are embedded in ascriptively defined regional and corporate kinship groups. Nonmembers of the RCAs who were corporately related were "morally and 'legally' obligated to make good the debts of a member. Should a member [of an RCA] default, die, or prove unable to repay his debts, his kin were expected to make good the obligation. Hence the credit of every participant in the rotating credit association was guaranteed by his family" (59–60). Default, fraud, or theft, was the exception. This was also true among Chinese *hui* in New Guinea (Wu 1974: 573).

On the other hand, Kurtz (1973: 53) has reported frequent cases of default among the *cundinas* in San Ysidro, and police in Tijuana reported cases of organizers absconding with the fund share. In fact, Cope and Kurtz (1980) have developed the thesis that organizers and participants in the RCAs take special care to include only certain trusted people in *tandas* because of the "concern with reducing the risk of default to a more acceptable level" (228). They do not, however, present any data on potential or actual default. Kurtz and Showman (1978) have stated that default was the most common problem in the *tanda*, but they do not present its frequency of occurrence. Although they report that the risk of default was not a serious consideration among *tanda* members, they also state that nonparticipants seemed to believe that *tandas* were poor investments because of the risks involved (69).

Out of over 60 informants from all the regions and cities of Mexico and the United States covered in this study, only 4 had experienced cases of default in the informal associations to which they belonged in which some sort of restitution was not made. When participants defaulted, they informed the organizer, sold their numbers to someone else, or found a replacement willing to make the contributions. Although two participants knew of cases in which an organizer founded an RCA, took the first number, and fled, there are few verified instances of default without restitution and fewer cases of fraud—the actual frequency of dishonesty among participants or organizers is extremely low. The notoriety of the occasional case of fraud or default results from the attention lavished on such cases by scandal magazines like *Alarma* (the Mexican equivalent of the American *National Enquirer*). While all informants admitted the possibility of fraud or default, most discounted the likelihood of it occurring. Widespread social and cultural parameters select against dishonesty.

Fixity and Density of Confianza

The rarity of actual fraud or default results from social and cultural dimensions that are as important as the individual evaluation of a person's reputation. Any individual's reputation is based on specific sets of relations and behavioral indicators of cultural legitimacy which attach members to statuses and contexts. It is from this attachment to statuses and contexts that the density of *confianza* is generated, and the uncertainty resulting from participating in economic relationships of some risk is lessened. While most Mexican communities north or south of the Rio Bravo do not have traditional regional and corporate kinship groups like the Japanese or Chinese to protect them from default or fraud, Mexican familial, occupational and residential networks and contexts attach people to statuses and generate binding reciprocal obligations that *function equivalently to corporate group obligations*. It is not fear of default (Cope and Kurtz 1980) that selects for fixity but, rather, for most *tandas vivas*, social demands initiated by the nature of reciprocal exchange and its underlying cultural construct of *confianza*.

Persons are attached to statuses by the internal density of the RCA and by the density of relationships outside the RCA, which are brought into the RCA and define the total density of the RCA itself. What must be recalled is that the most frequent number of participants in the RCAs is 10 and that such a number selects for greater density as expressed in the natural systems of the occupational, residential, and familial RCAs discussed. In other words, the RCA as an association becomes a "social fact" and operates not only according to the norms of the RCA but also in terms of all the relationships the members bring into the association from a variety of other contexts.

When, for example, an organizer is a member's aunt, the fixed relation of aunt and nephew makes the operation of the RCA much more certain. The density of relations among members, not just that between the members and the organizer, also solidifies the operation of the RCA. These two aspects of density, then, that created by the operation of the RCA as a social fact with its constituent activities such as the drawings, the shared meals, gift giving, visits, and exchanges of information; and that created by the multiplicity of relations brought into the RCA together with their probable density, fix members within the RCA and also reinforce relations established and operating in other contexts.

The probable density and the multiplicity of relations in a working-class residential rotating credit association in San Pedro, California, are illustrated in Figure 3.7. The diagram illustrates how people are not only attached within the association to the organizer but, from a variety of contexts, to each other. There are two kinds of density shown in the diagram. The first refers to the type of relationship that exists between each member and the organizer and between each member and the other members. These are five in kind: consanguineous, affinal, fictive, friendship, and occupational or residential. The second refers to the type of relationship in which there can be a differentiation of authority or prestige because of age. These relationships are of two sorts, dominant and equal. Not shown in the diagram is the relationship between any member and the organizer in regard to the operation of the RCA itself. These are of two sorts: "direct" transactions in which the organizer and a member have direct access to each other with regard to the collection or disbursement of funds, and "indirect" in which another member "plays" (*jugar*) for someone who is prevented by distance from participating. Indirect transactions are not common, but they can occur when the organizer and the surrogate member have established especially close *confianza*. The type of density is indicated by numbers and by broken or solid lines.

As can be seen from this RCA, the totality of the relations that can be brought to bear to lower the probability of default is impressive for most members. All persons are "fixed" within the association by something other than the financial transaction. Person D who is an "indirect" member with other people playing the number for her, has no fixed status with the organizer, but instead is fixed with three others within the association: C, E, and F. These three persons in turn are fixed affinally or by friendship in status relations with the organizer. As the organizer remarked in

Figure 3.7. Density of a Working-Class Urban *Cundina*
in San Pedro, California

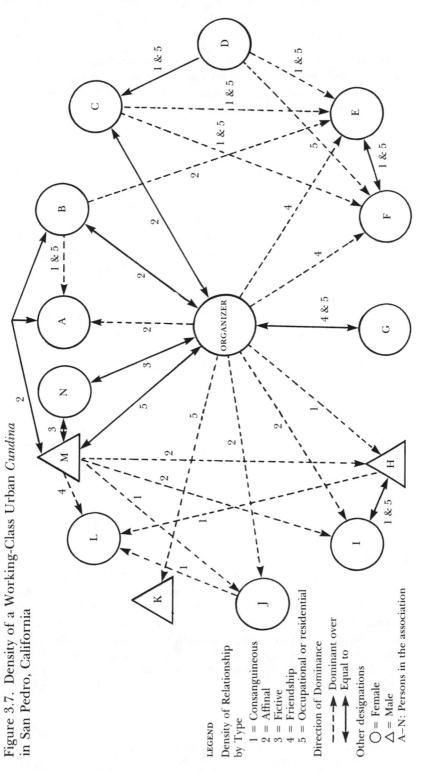

LEGEND

Density of Relationship
by Type

1 = Consanguineous
2 = Affinal
3 = Fictive
4 = Friendship
5 = Occupational or residential

Direction of Dominance

- - - → Dominant over
——— → Equal to

Other designations

○ = Female
△ = Male
A–N: Persons in the association

Source: Vélez-Ibañez 1980: 51.

commenting about the lack of direct connection with D, "The rest lend her mutual trust." The only other person without a direct fixed status with the organizer is L, but, like D, she is lent *confianza* by H, J, and M, as Figure 3.7 shows.

Safeguards

Other safeguards against default exist. I have already mentioned that many organizers will have access to the first turn if no fee is involved, which serves as a reserve in case members have difficulty with their contributions. Membership seniority is considered another safeguard, since those joining last probably receive the fund share last if no lottery system is used and thus pay in their share before receiving any money. In addition, in some institutional contexts, two other members of the RCA can witness delivery of the fund share, which safeguards against an organizer claiming falsely to have delivered it. These are among the obvious, explicit sorts of safeguards against uncertainty and the normal risk described by Light (1972). Certainly the cultural construct of *confianza* is congruent with the density and multiplicity of relations involved in RCAs and is insurance against indeterminate social relationships.

There are, however, in addition, cultural boundaries and behavioral expectations which on both sides of the Rio Bravo are used as a means to secure determinacy and fixity against the uncertainty of these economic relationships. North of the Rio Bravo, non-Mexicans, except for other Spanish-speaking populations or those considered equivalent to Mexicans, are excluded from participating in most RCAs.

However, three Anglo-American women in a Texas clothing factory who belonged to the same task section as the Mexican women had sufficient status to be asked to join. In another rare exception, Filipino workers in Chula Vista were invited to participate in Mexican *cundinas*. The rationale given by the Mexican workers was that Filipinos "*saborean de lo nuestro*" (they have our flavor). In this case, the Filipinos were regarded not as Mexicans but as culturally equivalent. Furthermore, Filipinos could participate with Mexicans in enjoying (*saborear* also can mean relish in the context in which this was stated) the conviviality of the RCA.

Cultural boundaries are not, however, generally relaxed for

non-Hispanic national groups. Informants pejoratively referred to Anglo-Americans as "gringos" when the question arose as to their acceptability as members. Blacks, unless they are Latin American, are regarded as *"duros"* (hard to get to know) and therefore not in the universe of probable candidates. Puerto Ricans, Panamanians, and other Central Americans who are also black are not only participants but organizers. These perspectives are reinforced by the structural conditions under which most Mexican residential, occupational, or familial RCAs operate in the United States. While occupations may have a cross-section of other nationalities and national minorities, cultural boundaries are usually replicated in the RCAs, especially in working-class or service-worker contexts. Residential and familial RCAs are equally closed owing to the social endogamy of both contexts.

On the other hand, there are class-specific behavioral expectations and clues within Mexican universes that operate as exclusive and inclusive boundaries. For example, among working-class women in Chula Vista, *pretenciosas* (pretentious women) are excluded because it is believed that such women will probably not pay their contributions on time. The rationale for this belief is that those who boast of their material belongings are likely to claim that they work for pleasure and not out of necessity. Such claims are deemed to be false and are thought to be a cover hiding economic problems and the lack of resources to meet social and economic obligations, including obligations to members of the *cundinas*. Even when such pretentiousness is not expressed, an individual's style of language may exclude him or her from consideration for *confianza*. University students, for example, who work during summer vacations may not be asked to join, not because they are temporary workers, but because they are generally regarded as only interested in intellectual topics and therefore outside of the discussion ranges of blue-collar workers. The fear is also present that such students will reject an offer to participate because of perceived class differences.

The qualities expected of a potential member in working-class sectors may include expertise in verbal dueling. *El cotorreo* or *la cábula* (literally "chatter," but analogous to "rapping" among blacks) is the main signaling device used to designate acceptance or nonacceptance, although general speech patterns and proxemic signals are also important. For example, a *cotorreo* about a sister is quite common, a sort of verbal gauntlet used by men in which one person will say "*¿Cómo está tu hermana?*" (How is your sister?), the other will ask, "*¿Cuál hermana?*" (Which sister?), and the first will respond with "*La que se acuesta en mi cama*" (The one who sleeps in my bed). Here the ending words rhyme in Spanish so that the challenge and responses are quite melodious. In addition, if a person is not given an individual nickname marking his personal appearance or some mannerism, he will usually be excluded. A new ceramic factory worker in Los Angeles was given the nickname of *Cebolla* (green onion). The rationale for his nickname was that he had white hair on top of his head but green roots in the lower extremities, as evidenced by his numerous amorous activities. Soon after he received his nickname, he was invited to participate in one of the *cundinas*.

Among women, joking patterns or nicknaming are also used to designate acceptance into *confianza* circles, especially in the working-class occupational RCAs. One woman member of an RCA in a San Diego electronics factory was known as *Teflón* because she was so dumb that nothing stuck to her. For both women and men, nicknames of a personal sort based on appearance, an infamous event, or a speech mannerism (one stutterer was known as *lenguas*, "tongues") indicate acceptance. Each marks the individual not pejoratively but in recognition of her or his individuality within the fellowship of a collective group.

In bourgeois sectors, where the clubs mentioned previously are active, numerous behavioral clues are observed before invitations are extended. Speech mannerisms that mark women as having rural or working-class origins eliminate candidates from clubs, even when they meet residential requirements. Class-specific dress, hairdos, access to automobiles, knowledge about certain types of entertainment, and assurance in certain behavioral patterns, like controlled laughter and emotion, are all used as class indicators in bourgeois sectors. In middle-class club RCAs in Monterrey, however, there are members whose working-class relatives participate secretly. In these cases, it is usual for the working-class relative to send money to her bourgeois relative in her bourgeois residential section by messenger. The messenger is often a young daughter. In this way middle-class sensibilities will not be offended since a young girl entering the front door of a middle-class home is not as conspicuous as a working-class adult. Of course the middle-class resident will not reveal to members of the club that she is in fact playing a lower-class relative's turn.

In some *tandas* far subtler clues than those so far described may be used. In the theater chains in Los Angeles a person who too readily agreed to participate in an RCA without questioning the operation, the cycle of payments and distribution, and the duration of the cycle, was generally perceived as not serious and therefore not a good candidate. Someone who accepted initial total *confianza* in the RCA without any analytical questioning could not be trusted to think on his own or convivially with others. As one informant put it, "One can be very certain, but not too certain, initially."

Such boundaries, safeguards, behavioral clues, and other cultural requirements, are not present nor are they needed in the well-established intermediate RCA and the formally organized *mutualista*. Since the former are integrated into a company's accounting system, it is difficult for employees to default on their contributions. There is always a possibility of accountant-organizers manipulating contributions, as has been indicated, but the risks involved are great, and dishonesty is rare. In the formal *mutualistas*, legal sanctions protect both the members and the organizers from either default or fraud, although given the reticence of the corporate officers to supply this research with data, there may be dimensions of the operation that were not made public. (These remarks are in no way intended to suggest any wrongdoing on the part of the corporation.)

Yet there are other uncertainties against which safeguards, fixed relations, and cultural boundaries are useless. Unexpected acts of men, women, and gods occur frequently enough to shatter confidence in the most well developed systems that are invented. The Mexican rotating credit association is no exception. Regardless of intentions, trust, fellowship, historical associations, ritual practices, density, multiplicity, protection, promises, cooperation, and cultural constructs, the sudden and unexpected appearance of inflation, the death of a relative, a lost or misplaced wallet, a sudden illness, an immigration raid, or unemployment—all mock intentions, and the safeguards against uncertainty melt away. At such times *confianza* may fail, old and treasured relationships may shatter, and personal uncertainty is confirmed by unexpected events. What has been determined by definition and practice becomes indeterminate by actions and accidents. It is at such times that an abuse of mutual trust can occur.

4 The Mutability of Social Life

UN ABUSO DE CONFIANZA (AN ABUSE OF MUTUAL TRUST): AN ETHNODRAMA

Most human transactions generate some bonds, as fleeting as those between customer and clerk in a grocery store or as determinate as those between intimate friends or relatives. Yet, once established, bonds cannot remain the same, although we like to think they do. The life cycle takes care of changes even among "permanent" relationships, such as those between children and parents. Bonds also have unintended and unforeseen consequences. A bond may initiate unintended and unforeseen spiraling actions, the final outcome of which may destroy the original bond and all the good intentions arising from the original exchange as well. Thus, the establishment of *confianza* or mutual trust is adaptive, but it is no guarantee against conflict, or the miscommunication of intentions. At the heart of the matter may lie such basic reasons as a species-specific trend toward learning "equivalences," but this is not the place for that discussion.[1]

Bailey (1971: 19) has offered an explanation for intimate conflict by stating that in the small-scale communities he studied, "those nearest are also those with whom you interact most frequently and, therefore, those with whom you are most likely to have a cause for contention." The seeming paradox that conflict may arise out of the closest and most intimate relationships is reminiscent of the dependent-independent conflict between parents and children developed in more psychoanalytic literature. This paradox, however, should not be understood as being based on the notion of proximity of frequency only. Rather, most people count on those closest to them the most, but nothing guarantees that even a brother can be relied upon when conditions beyond his control arise that negate even the most intimate bonds. In addition, however, it may very well be that the shame of being unable to fulfill the expectations of intimate relations causes a person to refuse assistance in harsh and unforgiving terms, and to use the most nefarious political tactics as a massive defense against distress that arises from wanting but being unable to fulfill expectations.

Such conflicts may also arise because relationships are so dense and multiple that expectations become too implicit and are not subjected to analysis. In other words, equivalent notions of events may be taken so much for granted and may be so embedded in dense layers of social relationships that intentions are misconstrued and motives misunderstood, and tragic errors accumulate that unravel treasured and valued relationships. That was so in this ethnodrama when the most intimate of friends reneged on a *tanda*. Such examples shed light on the mutability of determined relationships among people in contemporary urban industrial settings.

Finally, such paradoxes provide insights into the "emic" or insider views of such mutability and the uncertainty and indeterminacy generated by events. Indeterminacy and uncertainty are probably represented in all cultural systems by various constructs. In the Mexican case, the historical cultural construct of *chingar* (to screw or betray) has been cited in the literature as one such construct but from a perspective different from that assumed here. Paz (1961: 79) has suggested that the word defines a great deal of Mexican life and qualifies many of the relationships between Mexicans where manliness, strength, imposition, personalism, and a binary world made up of the strong and the weak are primary. Wolf (1959), in elaborating on the *Chingón* (the person), characterized the Mexican male who shares in such attributes by saying that the group only exists for the individual leader and that success is measured by the readiness of others to serve the individual. The *Chingón* (mestizo in Wolf's parlance) is basically trapped by the nature of his attempts to exercise power as a sexual projection. For Wolf these are not "national characteristics" but kinds of attributes related to those who hold and wield power.

From the point of view presented here, however, the construct of *chingar* is an emic explanation of disrupted *confianza* and not a motivator of social action. It is a construct that emerges as an insider explanation for dissolved relationships and for the constant mutability of social life. It is also differentially distributed in different social sectors. Among power holders, according to Wolf's description, the *chingar* construct explains the loss of power or threats to power. Among marginal populations, such a construct is used as an explanatory device to describe the economic and social conditions in which these populations reside. It is more than likely that such a construct will be less important as either an attributional guide or an explanatory device among middle-class sectors. Its usefulness to the populations sharing the construct is that it explains the unpredictable, the mutable, the indeterminate, and the uncertain. It is a type of ad hoc explanation which in a paradoxical manner reduces uncertainty by explaining the failure of *confianza* relationships. While mutual trust is expected, events generate pressures that may very well prevent such expectations from being fulfilled. When such events occur, they are explained in a subjective manner by the liberal use of *chingar*.

THE METHOD OF EXPOSITION

One of the best ways to sort out the paradoxes that make living so interesting is to couch analysis in terms of actors, place, and time. This is a handy method which allows the reader to participate in the reconstructed and observed events assembled by the anthropologist, which closely resemble the actual events. It is as faithful a rendition as possible, but still filtered by the reality of the observer-participant. It is thus somewhat selective of details but not designed to further an argument. This ethnodramatic approach works out as extensively and intensively as possible the various threads leading to a decision, the processes involved in the actualization of the decision, and the way in which the decision did or did not work for all of those involved in it.

Every ethnodrama unfolds within two necessary contexts: the first consists of the cultural constructs important from generation to generation that people use as references for decisions and actions. One of the dynamic qualities of such historical constructs is that they are distributed according to the social definition of such important realities as class, race, ethnicity, sex, age, physical condition, and individual personality. Thus historical constructs like *confianza* change when they are not efficacious, so that persons syncretize them, reinterpret them to suit conditions, or on occasion discard them—at least for a time. These constructs, then, are not the same for all, but groups of people will share close equivalents.

The second context consists of the structural conditions of econiches that are formed by geography, environment, and all the social categories mentioned like class and ethnicity. These structural conditions shape various behavioral environments and limit the range of possible actions. Thus, for example, those with more resources are more likely to have a greater opportunity to live out their lives' chances than those without.

All human drama, then, will be influenced and limited by the historical cultural constructs and structural conditions of a population, the implication of which is that no transaction or decision is ever "free." Neither of these elements, however, is itself immutable or without contradictions, paradoxes, and oppositions. The outcome for most of us is that actions or decisions are seldom ever tidy, but the search for tidiness continues, especially among social scientists.

Real-life ethnography, unlike the traditional account in anthropology, does not divide the material of living into subjects like economics, politics, ideology, and so on. Instead it presents the actors and their actions within boundaries defined by the participants rather than by the anthropologist's perceptions. Although tape and short-hand recordings, field notes, and systematic journal entries were used to reconstruct the events that follow, they were cross-checked with each participant, and verified by independent sources (others not present but with whom the participants shared information), multidimensional participation (taking roles other than that of observer, such as *tanda* member and recorder), and the actual observation of the rupture of the relationships described here.

The ethnodrama that follows is a rather untidy exposition because it reflects the often contradictory human element. It deals with Armando's network, discussed in Chapter 3. The reader should refer to that chapter for descriptions of the individuals involved and their relationships to the organizer. Two persons not mentioned previously but important to the ethnodrama are Florencia Loya, Armando's former lover, and Luis Benítez, Armando's friend and employee.

THE ETHNODRAMA

Dramatis Personae

tanda members	ARMANDO LÓPEZ, *tanda* organizer FELIPE LÓPEZ, Armando's intimate friend from the same rural area TOMÁS LÓPEZ, Armando's brother MRS. GUADALUPE LUNA, Tomás's mother-in-law GRACIELA LÓPEZ, Armando's sister MRS. CICOTE, Armando's next-door neighbor and also his younger sister's mother-in-law
non-*tanda* members	FLORENCIA LOYA, Armando's former paramour LUIS BENÍTEZ, Armando's employee and friend

The Place

Ciudad Netzahualcoyótl Izcalli[2]

Time

Seven and one-half months during 1972–1973

FLORENCIA FOOLS ARMANDO: ANTECEDENTS TO AN ABUSE OF MUTUAL TRUST. In 1971, Florencia, an attractive, intelligent, and vivacious 18 year old, became the center of Armando's amorous attentions. Florencia's grandparents had migrated to Mexico City in the twenties and had established themselves in one of the working-class areas; her father was a security guard. She had attended the local grammar schools and high school and finished her first year of *preparatoria*—an institution roughly analogous to junior college—in preparation for a career in nursing. Her aspiration to become a nurse was, however, cut short by her mother's illness, and she was forced to leave school. She devoted herself to taking care of her mother in the morning, and in the afternoon worked as a pharmacy clerk in one of the local drugstores, where eventually she met Armando.

Armando began to court Florencia seriously very shortly after they met because according to him, "lightning struck me." There were, however, several obstacles for Armando. First, a number of other suitors were also in competition. Second, Armando's economic situation was not stable. Shortly after he had met Florencia, his brother Tomás and his sisters Graciela and Virginia had migrated to Mexico City from Amtitlán, Puebla (a pseudonym). This placed an added burden on his already strained economic circumstances. Third, Florencia had been engaged to another man when Armando began to court her, and as a result Armando did not completely trust her.

Yet in spite of these obstacles, the courting began and shortly thereafter they became engaged. Further obstacles developed, however, when Graciela bore a child and Armando had to support both his sister and her infant. He purchased a small lot in Ciudad Netzahualcoyótl and constructed a *jacal* (small shanty) with a storefront so that his sister could support herself by selling groceries that he purchased in the Federal District. Over a period of six months he installed his sister and child in a three-room concrete block home, in the front of which he built a small area for a counter and an ice cooler for beer. This occurred without Florencia's knowledge, because her perceptions of Armando would have changed had she learned of his sister's illegitimate child.

During this period, Armando and Florencia's relationship was affected by his devotion to his sister's welfare. Armando spent less time courting Florencia than he did building his sister's home and storefront, and purchasing, delivering, and at times even selling groceries in Netzahualcoyótl. At the same time Florencia's former suitor began to call upon her again. He took Florencia to Netzahualcoyótl where he pointed out Armando's newly constructed shanty. This convinced Florencia that her future with Armando included the possibility of living in Netzahualcoyótl. Armando explained that the *jacal* was only for his sister but that he had also been busily building another home in the Netzahualcoyótl area which was not a *jacal*. Partially satisfied with this explanation, Florencia demanded proof of the "love nest" Armando had promised or the engagement would be called off.

During all this Florencia had not broken off her relationship with her former fiancee and thus was engaged to two men simultaneously. Late one evening, Armando saw them in her suitor's car and discovered how Florencia had found out about his sister's house in Netzahualcoyótl.

A short time afterward, Armando devised a strategy to avenge himself for Florencia's actions. He had set the stage for what was to occur when he had told Florencia that he was constructing another home for them in another neighborhood of Netzahualcoyótl. He contacted Felipe, who was finishing his own home in the same area of Netzahualcoyótl but without open sewer ditches and puddles of fly-infested stagnant water, then quite characteristic of many parts of the city. The house, a two-story concrete building, was partially finished and also partially furnished. He arranged with Felipe to have access to the home for a weekend and on a Sunday afternoon borrowed an automobile from another friend.

According to Armando, he took Florencia to his friend's almost finished home and claimed this was to be their love nest. Florencia swore undying love and affection for Armando, her only reservation being that the furniture in the house did not quite suit her taste. Armando stated that it was only temporary and that as soon as the building expenses were taken care of, new furniture would be ordered. He then asked for reassurances that they would marry and proceeded to try to make love to her which she initially refused, citing virginity and moral qualms about sex outside of marriage. Nevertheless, Armando persisted, claiming that he had proved his love and affection by building the home and that she had to reciprocate. Armando and Florencia shortly after this discourse spent the afternoon in love making.

In the late afternoon, Florencia asked Armando to return her to her home since her parents would be concerned. He refused, suggesting that she return by bus since he had no intention of driving back to Mexico City with a woman of questionable reputation. Florencia realized his strategy, and Armando proceeded to express his displeasure with her for her "unfaithfulness" with her former suitor and her unwillingness to sacrifice with him and share the initial difficulty of living in Netzahualcoyótl. He told her that her former suitor could now have back his slightly "soiled" fiancée. Armando left, Florencia took the bus, and they never saw each other again.

These events had occurred a year prior to the formation of the *tanda*. Whether the actions as described by Armando are entirely faithful reproductions of events does not matter. The point is that equivalent events probably occurred, or the abuse of *confianza* that took place during the course of the *tanda* could not have occurred.

SETTING UP THE *TANDA*: NEGOTIATIONS AMONG FRIENDS: CIUDAD NETZAHUALCOYÓTL. In Armando's storeroom behind his grocery store, Armando, Felipe, and Mrs. Cicote discussed who was to select the first numbers and how many each was to select. They had all agreed previously that the *tanda* was going to consist of 30 numbers with a weekly contribution of 100 pesos (for details on the operation of a similar *tanda*, see Appendix A). Felipe stated that he wanted numbers 1–6 and 26–30 since he wanted to buy more clothing for his business and the initial numbers would provide him with the necessary sum. Mrs. Cicote wanted numbers 1–3 because she needed the money to pay for tailored suits that she had ordered from Tomás. Armando wanted numbers 8–19, timing his share to come when he would have to make the last payment on his car and pay for repairs as well. Armando stated that Mrs. Luna did not care what numbers she was given and that she would not object to Mrs. Cicote having the first turns. He said that since Mrs. Cicote had already spent her portion by buying suits from his brother Tomás, it was only fair that she be given the first numbers.

Felipe objected strenuously that it was not his fault that Mrs. Cicote had spent her money and that he needed his as soon as possible. Mrs. Cicote stated that she could not afford to participate if Felipe received the money first since she was very short of cash. Armando said that the rest of the *tanda* members would be very disappointed if the *tanda* collapsed since they were already planning for it. At this point Felipe asked who the rest of the members were to be, and Armando responded that they were Tomás and Graciela. Armando said that Tomás wanted numbers close to the first turns since he was having a very difficult time with his tailoring business and needed the money to pay for cloth that he had ordered for Mrs. Cicote's suits. Armando also said that Graciela wanted numbers 10 and 11 to coincide with the Christmas holidays so she could buy gifts.

Felipe responded that since he was going to take 10 numbers and thus pay the largest amount, at least he should have the first 5 numbers. Armando countered that he too was going to take 10 numbers, run the *tanda*, and have all the headaches of collection and distribution. Yet he was willing to wait until the others received their money even though it would be very difficult because of the repair bills from his recent car wreck and the final payment on his car. Mrs. Cicote said quietly but forcefully that if Armando was willing to wait such a long time for his money so could Felipe. Felipe responded that he would have to forgo the "pleasure of the *tanda*" unless he at least began with the third turn, and the first 2 turns could go to Mrs. Cicote.

Armando summarized briefly by stating that Felipe's suggestion was acceptable and that Mrs. Cicote could take the first two turns (numbers 1–2), Felipe the next three (3–5), Tomás the next (number 6), and Mrs. Cicote turn 7. Numbers 8 and 9 were to be given to Graciela so that she would have money for gifts. Armando said that since he also needed the money badly he would then take turns 10–19, Mrs. Luna 20–23, and then Felipe could have 24–30.

Felipe objected that he did not consider it fair for him to "pay a vast amount of money" by taking the last seven turns. Armando said he understood how difficult things were with inflation, the rise of gasoline prices, and the upcoming holidays, and that he would take Felipe's last three turns and Felipe could take his turns 17–19. Felipe frowned at the suggestion but reluctantly agreed that the final suggestion was more equitable.

Thus the *tanda's* operation was finalized with the following distribution of numbers: Mrs. Cicote, turns 1–2; Felipe, turns 3–5; Tomás, turn 6; Mrs. Cicote, turn 7; Graciela, turns 8–9; Armando turns 10–16; Felipe, turns 17–19; Mrs. Luna, turns 20–23; Felipe, turns 24–27; and Armando, turns 28–30.

In the weeks that followed, all the *tanda* members faithfully carried out the agreement. Each person would go to Armando's store and deliver the money personally, the easiest procedure for all concerned. Since Tomás visited Armando's store nightly, Mrs. Cicote lived next door, and Graciela lived in the same household, collecting the money was never problematic. Occasionally, Mrs. Luna, Felipe, or Tomás would be late with the weekly contribution, but Armando as a favor would make up the difference and also turn over the fund share to the appropriate person. At such times, Armando would always reassure the delinquent person with his favorite phrase: "*No hay problema, somos de confi-*

anza" (No problem, we have mutual trust). Of course, each favor obligated the person beyond the obligation to make up the delinquent contribution.

In part, Armando's reputation within the extensive networks of his clothing business grew out of his generosity. Certainly the functioning of this *tanda* was assisted by his doing and having done favors. The *tanda* operation ran smoothly, then, until the twenty-eighth week.

EL ABUSO DE CONFIANZA. Armando waited throughout the Monday that began the twenty-eighth week for Felipe's arrival. Mrs. Cicote appeared early that morning, chatted with Armando for 15 minutes, drank two cups of Nescafé, and left her 300 pesos. Mrs. Luna dropped by in the afternoon and visited for a few hours during the course of which she turned over 400 pesos. Tomás dragged himself in at the end of the day to sip on a *caguama* ("turtle," referring to a turtle-shaped beer bottle). He delivered his 100 pesos without much prodding from Armando. Graciela had already turned over 200 pesos to Armando from the household account money that Armando provided her weekly.

For the next three days Felipe did not show up at Armando's house, nor did Armando see Felipe at the wholesaler's warehouse where they both purchased their clothes for resale. In addition, Luis who had begun to work for Felipe after leaving Armando's employ, had not shown up at the warehouse nor made his customary Wednesday visit to Armando's grocery store. Since Felipe's contribution of 1,000 pesos (10 numbers) was a considerable amount for Armando, he decided to visit Felipe. "Something," he suggested at the time, "very wrong must be happening to Felipe."

On the fourth day, Armando and I drove to Felipe's two-story home, the same house Armando had used the year before in his escapade with Florencia. Felipe's wife answered Armando's knock on the steel front door of the bare concrete building. She looked slightly embarrassed as she opened the door for, from the innards of the house, Felipe's voice could be heard bellowing out that he did not want to see anyone. She motioned to Armando and myself to enter and pointed the way to Felipe's bedroom. We both walked through the passageway, living room, and hallway to Felipe's bedroom. He lay on the bed with crumpled bedclothing strewn about, unshaven, and obviously not very pleased at our entrance.

He looked up and stated that he had been quite sick and had

not been able to get up for three days. Armando responded that he had been concerned because he had not seen him for three days nor had he seen Luis at the warehouse. He then asked Felipe what was happening. Felipe answered that he had been suffering from shortness of breath, headaches, unclear vision, and a high temperature. As he spoke, I noticed that he stuttered and that he spoke very rapidly and seemed to run short of breath with every sentence. He gulped and inhaled deeply.

Armando said that he had not seen Felipe in such a physical state in the years that they had known each other. Felipe answered that the worst part was that he felt a great deal of numbness in one leg and that, if he did not improve, he was not going to be able to collect from his customers. Armando said that he would do it for him and not to worry. Felipe responded that Luis had been taking care of it, leading Armando to ask why, if that was the case, Felipe was concerned about collecting the money owed to him. Felipe did not respond, and Armando asked him if he had collected enough for that week's *tanda* since he (Armando) had to make the last payment on his car.

Felipe still did not respond and rolled over on his side facing away from Armando. Armando repeated his question to which Felipe muttered to the wall alongside his bed, "*Ya no me estés chingando*" (Stop bothering me, or Stop fucking with me). Armando looked quite puzzled and said that this was a strange way for a buddy to treat him after all they had been through. Felipe told Armando to leave him alone and that Armando had not thought of all they had been through when they agreed to the selection of numbers for the *tanda*. He then turned away from the wall, threw off his bedcovers, and stood and faced Armando who stepped back slightly. Felipe screamed that he had told Armando from the very beginning that he needed the money in order to buy enough clothing for his business and that now he was faced with the prospect of not having enough clothing to sell for the holidays because he had to contribute the 3,000 pesos to the *tanda* (the total he owed for three weeks at 1,000 pesos per week).

Armando remarked that he could not help the way things turned out, and Felipe responded that he knew of the relationship with Mrs. Cicote and Armando's brother Tomás. He said that the fact that Tomás owed Armando for the bolts of cloth Armando purchased for him was important in Armando's decision to side with Mrs. Cicote initially. Since Mrs. Cicote would use her first turns to pay Tomás for the suits of clothing made her by Tomás, Tomás in turn could pay Armando the money he owed him for the bolts of cloth. This, Felipe screamed, was "*un abuso de confianza*," and that ever since then he had been sick to his stomach with all the symptoms he had described. He said in a screech that "*esto me duele hasta los talones*" (this hurts to the heels).

Armando replied that he had a clean conscience and that he had never meant to *chingar*, but that he had an obligation to the rest of the *tanda* members and they would not like Felipe reneging on the *tanda*. Felipe responded that he did not care and that Armando knew that the very house he was in had been used in a most particular way, and that some of the other members would certainly lose respect for him, especially the women. Certainly, he said, Mrs. Cicote would not be happy to participate in future *tandas* with Armando once she heard what he had done to Florencia. In addition, all the many women in his business route who had *confianza* in him would eventually also find out.

Armando stared briefly and quickly walked out, got into his car, and we sped away in silence. A second *abuso* had balanced out the first, or so it seemed.

AFTERMATH. Although the *tanda* continued to function for the next few weeks with the other members, the relationship between Armando and Felipe was severed permanently. Felipe for his part later stated that Armando's behavior in the *tanda* violated all of the intimacy required of the friendship relationship. Although he could understand a person feeling the obligation to ensure the welfare of his close consanguineous relatives by providing a small advantage so that they received the first few turns, he could not understand the violation of their long-standing friendship for personal gain. According to Felipe, Armando had been responsible for Felipe's successes in the clothing business, especially by making connections and establishing *confianza* relations with wholesalers. He said that they had come from the same town and shared the same surname, and had suffered together when they first arrived in Mexico City. Then they had had to sleep in the park and were urinated on by drunks who mistook them for sleeping dogs. Later, both participated in the same political protests in which they threw rocks at the local police and clashed with the state troopers over rights to their plot of land in Cuidad Netza-huacoyótl. Felipe said that he had even helped Armando over a personal matter of honor, and they had used his home to get even. Yet, Felipe said, "Armando treated me like a stranger, as if we had no mutual trust." By this he meant that Armando thought of his own welfare first, before that of their relationship and therefore in fact treated him like a stranger to whom there was no obligation. For Felipe, "*Se le pasó la mano a Armando*" (Armando went too far, but really meaning that he acquired too much power). As Adams (1975: 27) has suggested, "power is usually not thought to be an issue between two friends. Yet it is specifically to keep power from being an issue that friends often take extraordinary precautions to avoid even giving the appearance of manipulating or using coercion." By implication, Armando's manipulation of the *tanda* negotiations was not sufficiently cautious for Felipe.

AN INSIDE VIEW:
ARMANDO EXPLAINS HIMSELF

Armando and I sat in the small open patio of his concrete-block home sipping Superior beer in the late evening after I had spoken to Felipe about the conflict.

Anthropologist. Why did that happen with Felipe?

Armando. Because he is a cuckold (*Cabrón*) who does not respect friendship and intimacy. He left me holding the responsibility of paying for him, and that is what hurts me. If he had had economic trouble in not paying then I would not have minded but like that, like . . . (His voice trailed off).

Anthropologist. What do you mean?

Armando. Well, figure it out. I have to make up for what he did not put in, and it was my turn so I have to make up for what he had already collected which really belonged to me since it is my turn. That is what I mean. Now I do not know where that is going to come from since I have little space for these kinds of error. *Qué pinche son los amigos* (What fuckers friends are).

Anthropologist. All friends?

Armando. No, just some. But *confianza* is hard to keep and to believe in once something like this happens. *Un abuso de confianza.*

Anthropologist. From what Felipe said, and let me understand this right, you may have thought of yourself first. I do not say that, that is what Felipe said. What do you think?

Armando. That is stupid (becoming very angry). What did he do to me? Bringing up that business of honor and Florencia that you know about. How do you explain such things? That is really an abuse of mutual trust.

Anthropologist. That is true, but it does not concern me in the least, as you know. But it seems that for Felipe it was important because of what he said. He thought you had thought of only yourself in the selection of numbers.

Armando. I had not thought of it, I do not need money that badly. I had no use for Mrs. Cicote's money which she would have paid my brother. In the first place, my brother had paid for the bolts of cloth himself with his own money. I was doing a favor for Mrs. Cicote because I understand she was in worse trouble than we are [meaning Felipe and himself]. The car payment I can do by borrowing from my pals, and the car repair is not that bad.

Anthropologist. But I thought you said that was very important for you, and I am sure that Felipe thought so too.

Armando. I said that so that I could have the money in the middle of the association since things around us are so flexible.

Anthropologist. What do you mean so flexible?

Armando. I mean that everyday is a problem of establishing something that stays. I needed to be in the middle of the *tanda* so that I could be certain that those in the beginning and those at the end were with me.

Anthropologist. I do not understand.

Amando. To think on it, I do not either. But whatever the reasons, my intentions were never to *chingar* Felipe. His collection had been going well. I know that because we are in the same business. We buy together so that I do know what he sells and how much. He pays for what we charge on credit at the same time I do. He is not really in any kind of economic difficulty that is any more or less difficult than mine. We are all stepping on eggshells these days. But what he did to me was to try to use the past so that I do not say anything to the others. *Eso está chingado* (That's all fucked up).

Anthropologist. Maybe neither one of you had enough *confianza* in the other? What do you think?

Armando. How much is enough, these days? We are of the same blood, from the same pueblo, from the same roots, from the same suffering, and still this happens.

Anthropologist. Maybe that is why it happened.

Armando. You mean that we were too close?

Anthropologist. Maybe too close in some things and not in others.

Armando. That does not make sense to me. Either you trust in all things or you do not. He should have trusted me not to try to screw him—I would not have, and if he had felt that way, why did he not say something? (He paused, and looked at me.) Maybe he could not because he would have been ashamed to have brought it up. He thought he would have insulted me. He would have, you know, he would have insulted me for that which was never in my mind.

Anthropologist. Maybe that is why he felt so sick. He could not tell you, but he felt it and thought about it. But to think and feel that way was against all *confianza*, yet the way things seemed, it might have been easy for someone to think that, since all the claims people made pointed in a direction away from *confianza*. He could not tell you without insulting you, but he still felt very strongly, so he got sick. Maybe that is the only way he could figure the whole thing out.

Armando. Maybe so, but regardless, it is too late to do anything. It happened, and he used something he was not supposed to regardless of whose fault it was. We could never have *confianza* again. *Hijo de la chingada* (son of a whore).

COMMENTARY

El abuso de confianza was not one of intention or of strategy but, rather, the tragic result of the use of the language of claims. Each person in the *tanda* negotiations claimed to want access to *tanda* money for personal reasons. Armando who wanted money for his car, supported Mrs. Cicote but not for the reasons Felipe thought. She, on the other hand, claimed to need money to pay for services provided by Tomás to make sure that Armando would be paid by Tomás. She was not aware that Tomás did not owe Armando any money. This was another case of altruism, much like Armando's toward Mrs. Cicote. Armando also wanted his sister to have money for the holidays, and Tomás money to pay his debts. His own motives in the negotiations were not quite as egoistic as they at first seemed. He sought protection for himself not just by making sure he received funds generated by others, but also by "being in the middle" of the RCA. As he said, "I needed to be in the middle of the *tanda* so that I could be certain that those in the beginning and those at the end were with me." He was the leader of the *tanda*, but he also wanted to be part of the association of equals. On the other hand, Felipe thought that when Armando sided with Mrs. Cicote, he was investing more in his own welfare than in the relationship between them. Felipe could not, however, articulate that belief without endangering their entire relationship. By protecting their *confianza* and not bringing up his feelings, Felipe contributed in an unintended manner to his own illness and the eventual rupturing of *confianza*.

Most of the principals acted not out of any egoism of the moment but rather out of a sense of *confianza*; in a situation of unquestioned trust they felt obliged to claim need. Armando trusted Felipe to understand that he was indeed extending himself to Mrs. Cicote and believed that in fact Felipe could handle the last turns of the *tanda* since Armando trusted him to be most able to withstand the rigors of being paid last. Those who received first were least able to pay. Those who from Armando's point of view could withstand the stress of saving throughout the *tanda* were those with whom the greatest confidence was shared. The fact that he as organizer had the right to take the first number but placed himself last to follow Felipe, illustrates his acceptance of Felipe as an equal worthy of the kind of trust he would have in himself.

In this ethnodrama, the bonds of *confianza* prevented the airing of possible problems or misunderstandings. Instead, the depth of mutual trust militated against the possibility of any of the principals making decisions in any other manner. Such dense relations are sensitive to displays of pressure. Indeterminacy can arise from the most determined of cultural inventions and constructs, including *confianza*, and it is from such disrupted *confianza* that a counter-construct such as *chingar* can emerge. But perhaps this paradox in which indeterminacy arises from determined social relations that are multiplied and densely glued by *confianza*, by pushing Mexicans, like other human populations, toward an expansion and adaptation of human consciousness beyond historically established and structurally related constructs, is also more selective in the long run. Ethnodramas like *"Un Abuso de Confianza"* are, however, infrequent, and the RCA is quite selective for positive consequences in a variety of contexts.

5 The Multidimensional Adaptations of Rotating Credit Associations

THEORETICAL ASSUMPTIONS

Rotating credit associations are cultural forms that produce a variety of positive intended and unintended consequences for those who engage in them. That is, according to the specific context in which participants engage in such practices, RCAs will benefit them by fulfilling or increasing the probability of fulfilling sociocultural and biological needs. Rather than assuming a perspective in which a cultural form is adaptive when it contributes to the success of a population in competition with other groups in an environment (Wu 1974: 567; cf. Cohen 1968), I consider a cultural form as adaptive when its consequences increase the probability of socioculturally or biologically defined needs being met in diverse circumstances. In fact, the diversity of the consequences a cultural form has generated will probably contribute to its maintenance within a sociocultural system. This means that the same cultural form will not have precisely the same adaptive consequences for different populations in various contexts, but rather that a form is adaptive because in fact it is congruent with the many variable needs of the various populations who use it.

Rotating credit associations are adaptive for the poor and the wealthy, the working class and marginal groups, professionals and blue-collar workers, women and men, the elderly and children. Each of these heterogeneous sectors has a variety of differentially distributed and culturally defined needs generated by the contexts in which these populations reside. RCAs are adaptive because they help meet the needs each population has defined as essential to its continued existence. The cultural form of the RCA does not define the needs to be fulfilled, but rather, like any other cultural invention, remains viable and important for behavior because of its flexible potential in diverse contexts.

CLASS AND CONTEXT

Marginal Sectors

From an examination of the various social and economic sectors in which RCAs appear, their adaptive flexibility can be appreciated. Both Kurtz (1973) and Lomnitz (1977) have described in detail the manner in which RCAs are used in areas where economically marginal populations predominate. Lomnitz, for example, has shown that in Cerrada del Cóndor, a shantytown of about 200 houses in Mexico City, the *tandas* are closely connected to the residents' reciprocity networks. According to Lomnitz the *tandas* represent an "important system of economic cooperation" which functions to limit the risks of saving money under mattresses, prevent premature spending of available resources, provide a practical way for groups to save in a situation in which the opportunities for individual savings are limited, and reinforce the level of *confianza* among the members of the *tanda* and the networks from which they are recruited (1977: 89). Lomnitz states that individuals can successfully counter the basic uncertainty of a marginal existence by generating methods of economic solidarity that mobilize available resources efficiently. Among many other mechanisms, RCAs are very important material mechanisms by which a marginal existence can be manipulated. The social wealth of networks can be exploited to allow limited material wealth to be used by as many as possible without waste and without creating further impoverishment.

My data on marginal sectors in Ciudad Netzahualcoyótl Izcalli and Los Angeles indicate that persons of limited means have to pay exorbitant rates of interest to purchase consumer goods on credit. By belonging to RCAs, they can accumulate sufficient savings to purchase these goods and by eliminating interest payments, avoid further marginalization.

For those in marginal sectors, RCAs serve yet other functions. By providing the wherewithal to purchase gifts and commensal items, they enable people to meet crucial ritual obligations. As Figure 2.9 shows, fulfilling ritual obligations, such as those of *compadrazgo*, was the second most frequent (17%) use of RCA funds. Meeting such ritual obligations in fact expands helping

networks and increases social wealth. Accumulating money to meet
such obligations selects for an increased number of social links
and, with that increase, access to more favors. Each favor represents the possible reduction of a price in the marketplace, an increase in the number of tortillas received for a given expenditure,
reduced prices in a clothing store, a discount on shoes, an introduction for a job, assistance in taking care of children, advice on
medicine for a sick child, information about a desirable medical
practitioner, the intervention of a political figure when a family
member is jailed, access to a social security number and green
card, or simply information about whom to avoid on a particular
day. Each favor in turn is eventually returned. RCAs contribute
to the continuation and expansion of such reciprocal networks and
thus increase the probability of cultural and biological needs being
met under conditions of extreme scarcity. In marginal contexts,
cooperation, not competition, selects for individual and group
survival.

Working-Class Sector

Within working-class sectors, RCAs have similar expansionary
social consequences. Although economic conditions are, of course,
more comfortable than in marginal sectors, access and reciprocity
still increase as a consequence of meeting ritual obligations. On
the other hand, RCAs play crucial roles in occupational processes
within working-class sectors, both service and industrial. In the oil
fields of Veracruz, for example, those engaged in *tandas* are for
the most part regular, long-term employees. They are highly
skilled, well paid, industrial workers, protected by a very strong
labor union. Their fringe benefits are the envy of the other industrial workers of Mexico. In the oil fields *tanda* participation is restricted to this regular work force, which keeps out the transient,
temporary field worker who is hired when production demands
increase the need for labor. Thus the elite status of the regular
field worker is to some extent enhanced by his *tanda* membership.

Among ceramic factory workers in West Los Angeles, various
mechanisms are used to accumulate funds, including lotteries,
games of chance, and the *cundinas*. Like the oil workers' *tandas*
these *cundinas* accentuate the elite status of certain workers. A $50
deposit, returned at the end of the *cundina*, is required, and only

those whose wages are high enough can afford such an entrance fee. For both the oil workers of Veracruz and the ceramic workers, *tandas* and *cundinas* contribute to greater social density between workers, but they also as an unintended consequence, reinforce certain elitist patterns.

Yet even the ceramic workers, like the marginal populations, suffer from factors of uncertainty and indeterminacy. For these workers, immigration raids are a constant source of uncertainty and a real threat to durable relationships. While economic stresses are felt by such workers, especially since there is little formal union organization, their skills are highly specialized and therefore in great demand. Factory owners are quite content to protect their workers' wages and offer benefits in some ways superior to union-organized factories. Thus the *cundinas* serve not just as a monetary cushion for the ceramic workers, but as a mechanism of solidarity among them, especially those disturbed by immigration raids.

The consequences of RCAs for workers in labor-intensive industries like clothing manufacture are different from those in highly skilled craft sectors. Among clothing workers in the near sweatshop factories of El Paso or Los Angeles, the competition for overtime piece work is intense. Such competition takes place within sections devoted to such specialized tasks as riveting jeans or attaching zippers, and involves relatively large numbers of workers. Because assembly-line methods are used in the very large factories, such as Farah or Tex, competing workers must of necessity work side by side. It is likely that members of the same task section will cooperate in the operation of the *tanda* or *vaca* (in El Paso). Thus while the total structure of the factory demands incessant competition for overtime privileges between members of the same task section, the RCA serves as one of the few means by which cooperation is generated. It thus acts to overcome the stress brought on by that competition and the low hourly wages. Its success in achieving solidarity can be measured by the fact that it was within such task sections that the few non-Mexican or Hispanic members also participated in RCAs.

Professional and Middle Sectors: Women, Men, and Clubs

Within residential and occupational middle sectors, the specific context determines the variable consequences of RCAs. Married

women basically rely on the household allowances they receive
from their husbands for their contributions to RCAs, but by their
participation they create circumstances in which they can spend
money as they wish, that is, on other than household items. Relationships between middle-sector wives and husbands, like those
between working-class and marginal-sector wives and husbands,
are characterized by dependency. The husband's generosity in
setting up his wife's allowance influences his power over her. The
RCA enables wives to feel more secure and mitigates some of the
uncertainty of dependence. Many women commented that "there
is nothing like one's own" to enable one to make a decision, comparing this freedom to the constraints they felt in their role as dependent housewife. In some of the interviews, in fact, husbands
were quite surprised to learn that their wives engaged in the
RCAs. Some women kept their participation totally hidden, citing
their husbands' propensities to influence the expenditure of the
fund share.

Yet there were important consequences beyond the individual
level for such sectors. RCAs allowed many households engaged in
living beyond their means in a consumer, credit-based context,
to get through the month without increasing their debts. As a consequence, some equilibrium between resources actually available
and debts was achieved. Such stasis, although it did not resolve
the basic problem of indebtedness, did alleviate stress within the
household. It was not unusual for middle-sector husbands to belong to occupational RCAs and their wives to participate in residential ones. The combination of the two RCAs allowed couples
to keep their heads slightly above water and in this way reduced
uncertainty.

There are still other consequences in middle-sector contexts.
For some middle-sector women removed by a job or marriage
from a working or marginal sector, many consanguineous, affinal,
and fictive relationships have been strained, if not disrupted, by
changing values and the acquisition of *pretenciosa* (pretentious) respectability. *Pretenciosa* is the cultural construct used by those
from other sectors to describe the middle sector. The construct
describes the disengagement of such persons from relatives and
friends in working- or marginal-sector networks. Visits between
relatives become episodic, gift giving becomes haphazard or mechanical, and ritual obligations are seldom met between class-

divided relatives. The result for many such women is the impoverishment of historical familial or friendship networks (see Vélez-Ibañez 1978b).

The RCAs serve as important mechanisms enabling such women to associate with other women and generate "fictive friendships" (Moore 1978: 63). The usual pattern is for 20 or so women to gather on Friday afternoons between 4:00 and 8:00 to share information on children, husbands, households, television programs, and neighborhood improvements or changes. Besides providing the setting in which to distribute and collect funds for the *tanda*, these socially crucial meetings anchor women with others of the same sector in an association that functions in a manner somewhat reminiscent of the primary group relations disturbed by class changes. The consequences of such associations for these women go much beyond the intended club activities, creating for them equivalent reciprocal obligations normally found in primary relations. There is little doubt, as an ample literature shows[1] and data from this research verify, that structurally changed contexts stimulate people to seek out voluntary associations. In the aftermath of vertical mobility and the resultant value changes, people construct fictive relationships with others. The idiom of friendship is used, but interaction is sparse. Thus although these relationships seem to have attributes of friendship, they do not carry with them density, reciprocity, and affect, except in the context of *tanda* and club.

Affective needs fulfilled before class change by kin and long-term neighbors can probably no longer be satisfied by them because of class differences and perspectives. Yet affective needs, especially those involving personal security, can seldom be fulfilled by material success or upward vertical mobility alone. The club and fictive friendships provide some measure of personal security and new relationships based on the middle-sector value of conspicuous consumption. The RCA's money-rotating mechanism allows this value to operate, but at the same time it guarantees flexible, mobile associational relationships. The very practice reinforces middle-sector values of consumption, but also integrates those values into a network of mobile and easily transferable social relations, which themselves demand such values symbolically and concretely. The same sort of congruence between values and network relationships is generated among upper-class women

by the RCA, except that the basic value articulated and integrated by such practices is not conspicuous, but rather sumptuous,
consumption.

There are, however, other important consequences for such
sectors. Among relatively high-level administrators in the Mexican
national social security system, it was not unusual for RCAs of
large amounts to be tied to office politics. These administrators'
budgets were supervised by politically appointed bureaucrats, and
each administrator was in direct competition with the others for
budget allocations. The allocations served as signals the administrator could read to determine the political strength of his competitors. Yet at the same time all these competitors participated in
the same RCA.

Membership in an RCA itself, however, was also read as a
signal of a competitor's strength. Since budgets were a well-kept
secret between the supervisor and each administrator, an administrator who did not participate in the RCA was considered to be
in disfavor. The reasoning behind this belief was that a person in
disfavor could not afford a high-priced RCA and could probably
not finish the full turn of a year-long RCA, which most of these
were. The consequences for administrators participating in the
RCA were positive, since a participant was likely to be regarded
as being in control of his domain and in favor with the supervisor.
For those not so regarded, further budget encroachments and
more devastating office politics resulted. On the other hand, there
were administrators with political acumen who were in disfavor,
but sacrificed a great deal to maintain their contribution to the
RCA. By obscuring their true circumstances, they kept competitors off balance.

The RCAs had yet other important consequences. Although
the administrators were competitors in one context, as members
of an RCA they cooperated in their obligatory relationships. Such
cooperation crosscut divisions of competition and created alliances
between departmental administrators and others in the struggles
over budget allocations. The RCA assisted in integrative functions
beyond those intended by its participants. Most institutions do
operate not only according to the bureaucratic rules that define
them, but also according to informal mechanisms like the RCA.
The RCA in this case served to stimulate crosscutting ties in one
context—that of its own operation—and to loosen them in an-

other—that of political competition. This "tying and untying" process is one means by which the social relations within the institution operate and, as an unintended consequence, provides a dynamic impetus for the operation of the institution itself.

Networks of the Elderly

Among networks of elderly retired bourgeois men and women in Mexico City, *tandas* are anchored in recreational activities. Canasta, pinochle, excursions, painting classes, museum visits, operas and symphony concerts, library visits, and occasional group vacations fill finishing life cycles. For the most part, such persons have accumulated durable relationships and social credits which they draw on during such recreational activities (Moore 1978). Social relations are expressed in shared laughter at the past and in favors such as cheating for the other during canasta games or buying popcorn for the other in a theater or park. These activities are anchored not only by accumulated social credits and durable social relations but by the common reality of these individuals being near the end of their lives. The *tanda* provides material proof of the durable reciprocity of present and past relationships. *Tandas* commit those at the end of the life cycle to the future by placing in the distance the obligation to reciprocate by contributions. While the uncertainty of the future is made real by the deaths of those around them, their investment in the future, masked as an obligation, contradicts that uncertainty.

For the elderly in these bourgeois networks the life cycle has also meant some withdrawal from interdependent relations with younger cohorts. Such networks are marked by their members' relative independence from either the economic or social necessity of maintaining dependent or interdependent relations with children, grandchildren, or institutions controlled by the young.

This is not the case for working-class or marginal-sector elderly persons who participate in *tandas*, for unlike the elderly bourgeois, they do not generally join age-homogeneous *tandas*. For the majority of the working-class and marginal elderly, interdependence with the young—children, grandchildren, or friends—is necessary for most endeavors. One consequence for the working-class and marginal elderly is that interdependent relations between different age groups is maintained, thus preserving a sense of continuity throughout the life cycle.

Institutional Contexts

The complex reciprocal obligations generated among female civil service workers have already been mentioned (see "Joining and Recruitment," Chapter 2). In these offices gift giving, commensal activities, and economic cooperation through the *tandas* replicate "normal social relations" (Goffman 1961: 6). New employees entering such offices are integrated into the local-level complex of relationships outside of the normative authority or power relations defined by the institution. Integration into the actual dynamics of social action within such partial institutions is made easier, and such integration softens the stresses created by the uncertainty of a new context. Group obligations of reciprocity between old and new employees are generated in such contexts, so that political relations between those with seniority and those without it are equalized by the *tanda*, gift-giving, and commensal obligations.

While persons in such contexts are separated by authority, seniority, and responsibility, the other relationships crosscut such divisions and create greater solidarity among the women. While hierarchy divides, the fact that each member of the *tanda* whose turn it is to receive the fund share is also responsible for collecting, makes necessary the recognition of equality by all concerned.

In institutional settings, whether private or public, in which employees from different task sections or departments participate in the same RCA, divisions created by the administration of such tasks are crosscut by the RCA relations. Even the highly specialized departments in the Museum of Anthropology, each of which has its own head (*maestro*), are crosscut by the RCAs. Heads of sections organize *tandas* and include participants from other sections. Such RCAs also serve as information conduits between the sections, enabling them to share information on their budgetary and resource restrictions. The maintenance of a repair and construction schedule is sometimes dependent upon the information channels kept open by the RCAs or other reciprocal mechanisms.

In a more general sense, such crosscutting ties and dense interactive networks increase the probability that information about an institution will be exchanged. In this way employees improve their positions relative to opportunities that arise in other offices. According to informants in institutional offices, since wages for lower-level office workers in most public and private institutions are very low, employee turnover is high. Changing jobs within the institution is, however, positively regarded since relations can be maintained across office cleavages. The information exchanged during the workings of the *tandas* and other reciprocal mechanisms does provide a guide to probable intra-institutional opportunities. Thus institutions in which *tandas* and other reciprocal mechanisms are present tend to retain their employees and greater employee solidarity is created.

GENERAL ECONOMIC CONSEQUENCES

I have suggested that for marginal, working-class, and middle sectors, general scarcity of means and living beyond one's means are two important conditions under which the RCAs are adaptive. In eliminating interest charges from market relations, RCAs of the informal or intermediate types are also highly adaptive. Some of the most conspicuous examples of such interest-free consequences occur in the VW or Datsun *tandas*. It should be recalled that since 40 persons are engaged in accumulating 88,000 pesos per month to purchase a car for cash, and then by lottery selecting the person to receive it, a substantial saving in interest is a primary consequence. Since the interest on cars over a 40-month period is almost 88,000 pesos, *tanda* VWs save each participant that amount. Such a substantial saving in fact frees the participant to engage in other economic strategies that could enhance his or her position.

There are, however, other consequences of note that should be discussed. First, the fact that people are willing to delay gratification, possibly for 40 months, by saving 88,000 pesos without any immediate reward is remarkable. The willingness to delay gratification for such a long period certainly testifies to the application of the *confianza* construct in situations extending beyond the highly dense networks of relationships, in which it normally appears. Al-

though it is understood that there is a 1 in 40 chance that an individual will in fact be selected as the first VW owner, there are also
39 chances that he or she will not be. Although one's chances improve each time another car is allocated, the reliance on chance to
turn up an earlier delivery expresses a willingness to delay gratification. It is in fact a remarkable achievement for such persons to
invest so much *confianza* in the informal mechanisms allocating
the automobiles and in those who are administratively in charge
of the effort. Greatest, however, is the *confianza* in themselves to
put off ownership until luck decides in their favor. In this case,
economic maximization comes from avoiding interest charges; the
participants gamble on winning first, but because they are willing
to delay gratification for as long as the lottery system dictates, the
bet seems like a sure thing—there is no way to lose. In a sense,
the participants are investing in their own self-control and disci-
pline. Most RCAs generate this same self-discipline not to spend,
and most do it within an obligatory savings relation.

There are two other contexts in which the activities of participants seem noneconomic in the formalist sense.[2] In informal and
intermediate RCAs in which the first turn is free, zero is taken,
or a fee is charged, the participants put in more than they take
out of the RCA. I mentioned previously that such commercialized
RCAs accounted for 42 percent of the dollar and peso RCAs
sampled. The question arises whether persons in marginal, working-class, or debt-ridden bourgeois sectors, do not in fact participate in nonadaptive RCAs since their already strained resources
are further decreased by the fees paid to the organizer.

The answer seems to lie in part in the uncertainty of the context and not in the economic gain. For the most part, fees are
charged in residential RCAs and not in familial or occupational
ones. RCAs appear frequently in areas of high population mobility. Since one of the major adaptive consequences of participation is the creation of reciprocal obligations, in a mobile context
the associations select for greater social stability rather than material gain. Second, highly mobile populations are likely to be alien-
ated from institutional sources of credit or savings since they
are unlikely to have established a credit rating.

For populations that are not highly mobile, the consequences
can also be adaptive. The organizers' fees are in fact no higher

than the value of the service they provide. Because the organizers usually collect the members' money personally, the members are at least assured of visits from the organizer and are offered the opportunity to establish personal relations with others. As informants have suggested, the relief of not having to expend energy in dressing children, feeding them before departure, arranging the household, and paying for transportation to a savings institution, is a fair exchange for the fee paid.

For the corporate *mutualistas*, the intended and unintended economic consequences are positive adaptations. First, the payments are scheduled in a manner that makes it relatively convenient for people in many class sectors to have access to accumulated sums. Given the procedures necessary to establish credit in most lending institutions, it is easier, even though collateral is required, for an individual to be an acceptable member of a *mutualista* than a customer in a lending institution. The corporation of *mutualistas* accepts members more readily than do lending institutions. Second, for the member there is a chance of paying less than what is received, thanks to the lottery system. In *mutualistas* with 40 members, there are 20 chances that a person will pay more than he or she receives, and 20 chances that a person will pay less than what he or she receives. The economic consequences are distributed according to chance, with a 50-50 probability that more will be received than contributed (and vice versa). Yet a third consequence is that each person has the same possibility of becoming a borrower, although he or she will have to pay for the privilege of getting the fund share earlier. Each person also has the same possibility of becoming a lender and profiting thereby. In essence each person, in order to improve life's chances becomes a risk taker. This single ingredient can in the long run be relatively adaptive in most urban environments. (In addition, of course, the participant is protected by the corporation's death and accident benefits.) Like deutero-learning of saving, taking risks in the *mutualistas* over extended periods generates a type of deutero-learning of risk taking, which is positively selected for in most urban environments. The last consequence of participating in such *mutualistas* is access to accumulated capital, which in times of inflation does not cost as much as the charges for having the first allotted number would as first suggest.

INTERSTITIAL CONSEQUENCES
AND DIMENSIONS

One of the most difficult tasks in anthropology has been to tie together analytically various levels of social domains. Wolf (1956), for example, pointed in that direction when he stated that anthropologists might properly concentrate their analytical energies on the interstitial connections between various levels of social action in complex social systems. Brokers, for example, are one such interstitial connection that has been studied by a variety of commentators (Bailey 1969; Blok 1974; Boissevain 1974; Fallers 1965; González 1972; Vélez-Ibañez (1978a).

Another interstitial connection is that made among various domains by the use of rotating credit associations. Regional interstices, like those between Guadalajara in central Mexico and such northern border towns as Ciudad Juárez, are bridged by merchant connections. RCA money collected in Guadalajara is used as working capital for merchants who buy used American clothing in El Paso, which they sell in Guadalajara at a substantial profit. That same profit is used by the merchants to pay contributions to RCAs not just in Guadalajara, but in El Paso and Juárez as well. The costs of purchasing clothing in El Paso and passing it through customs are made less burdensome by the fact that expenditures on lodging and meals are minimal since the merchants stay with relatives with whom *tanda* (*vaca* in El Paso) relations are also established. (It is interesting to note that the merchants who participate in RCAs in Guadalajara, Juárez, and El Paso must also be able to shift nomenclature from *tanda* in Guadalajara, to *quiniela* in Juárez, to *vaca* in El Paso, which illustrates the basic similarity of all RCAs.) Moreover, the regional gaps between central Mexico and the northern border areas are connected not only by the trade efforts of such merchants but by the extension of *confianza* between networks of people in entirely different regions.

International interstitial connections, generated by commuter *cundinas* which probably appear in almost every border region between Mexico and the United States, are more direct. As I have indicated, these commuter *cundinas* are tied to the exchange rates, and the choice of currency depends on the participants' projections of fluctuations in the exchange rate between dollars and pesos. All concerned review the daily transactions on the monetary exchanges in order to ferret out any long-range trends. Their goal is to produce a profit by exchanging a dollar fund share for pesos or vice versa.

Most commuter *cundinas* are basically informal, with the organizer living in Mexico and the members in the United States. Needless to say, this kind of connection across national borders has to be based on quite well-established *confianza* networks. The bridging of local-level interstices by commuter RCAs has yet to be explored in depth.

Among the most important interstitial connections are those between different social levels of activity and organization. Connections between local-level kinship networks, institutional contexts, residential sectors, and class sectors are illustrated in Figure 5.1, which shows the kinship network of a couple in Monterrey. Included are José and Rosa López and their children, Ramón, Elías, Ana, Olea, and Evita. Each of the five children in turn has children, whose names are omitted, except for Olea's Petra and Elías's Rosa and Elías, Jr. The diagram also shows the spouses of each of the five offspring and the connecting link to a second familial network of the same generational cohort: the Listo network.

The Listo network, all of whose members live in the squatter settlement of Colonia Paraíso, begins with Yspírito and Polo. Yspírito is a sister of Regina who is Ramón López's wife. Thus the affinal relationship between Regina and Ramón extends to the Listo network. Yspírito and Polo have seven children, Johnny, Norma, and five others not shown. Johnny has established intimate friendship and *compadre* relations with a third network composed of Carenas and Carlotta. As will be seen, each of the three networks is also connected to the others and to institutional sectors through *tanda* participation.

Each of these networks, however, is also representative of different residential and class sectors. The López parents are basically working-class persons who live in a residential area outside of Monterrey called Viste el Valle. The area is generally inhabited by working-class people who are employed year round, have relatively steady incomes, and have purchased homes constructed of relatively high-quality materials. Both José and Rosa participate in a joint *tanda* with their daughter Olea who lives nearby with her children and four of her husband's by a previous marriage. Olea,

Figure 5.1. Interstitial Connections

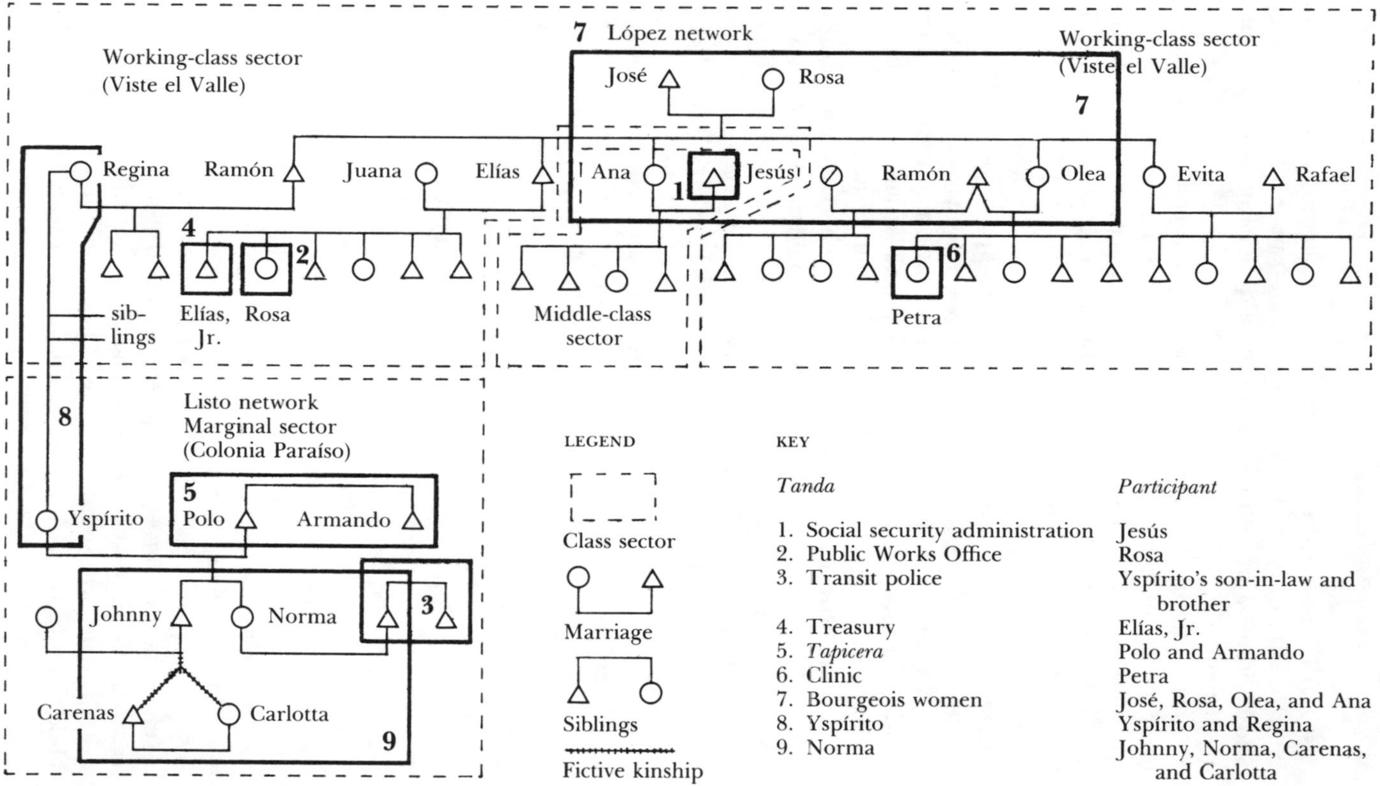

Working-class sector
(Viste el Valle)

Working-class sector
(Viste el Valle)

López network

Middle-class
sector

Listo network
Marginal sector
(Colonia Paraíso)

José   Rosa   Evita   Rafael

Ana   Jesús   Ramón   Olea

Petra

Regina   Ramón   Juana   Elías

Elías, Rosa
Jr.

siblings

Yspírito

Polo   Armando

Johnny   Norma

Carenas   Carlotta

LEGEND

Class sector

Marriage

Siblings

Fictive kinship

KEY

Tanda	Participant
1. Social security administration	Jesús
2. Public Works Office	Rosa
3. Transit police	Yspírito's son-in-law and brother
4. Treasury	Elías, Jr.
5. Tapicera	Polo and Armando
6. Clinic	Petra
7. Bourgeois women	José, Rosa, Olea, and Ana
8. Yspírito	Yspírito and Regina
9. Norma	Johnny, Norma, Carenas, and Carlotta

José, and Rosa all share a number in a *tanda* that is part of Ana's bourgeois residential sector. Ana is the wife of a medical doctor and acts as the broker for her parents and sister in the residential *tanda* in which only bourgeois women participate.

This example is extremely important for it points to the generalization of class divisions produced by a job or marriage within the Mexican population. Ana's relations with all of her brothers and sisters, as well as with her parents, are strained. Visits are rare, José and Rosa serve as caretakers for Ana's home when she and her husband go on vacation, and ritual exchanges are mechanical and lack spontaneity. Yet José, Rosa, and Olea, all working-class, faithfully share in Ana's contribution to her bourgeois *tanda*. The interesting aspect of this participation is that Ana discriminates against her relatives socially. This can be seen not only in their strained social relations, but also in the fact that Olea's daughter Petra, whom Ana describes as young, well-dressed, and nice looking, is the only one allowed to deliver the *tanda* contribution to Ana's home. Thus although José, Rosa, and Olea cannot participate in Ana's *tanda* directly because of class restrictions, Ana is assisted by their participation. Since the contributions are sizable, Ana could not seriously contemplate participating by herself. Her husband's medical career has always been with the national health service, and he therefore does not have an income equal to that of other husbands in the area. It may well be, however, that many other women who have joined such class sectors relatively recently also participate by cooperating with working-class relatives in order to enhance their bourgeois standing, though I have not verified this proposition. Because José, Rosa, and Olea participate in the same *tanda* with Ana, kinship exchanges across classes are made possible. So, too, do Petra's visit and collection of money establish social connections across geographic differences. While geography and class separate, kinship and *tanda* reciprocity cross-cuts cleavages and differences.

Such interstitial connections also extend from working-class sectors to marginal sectors. Regina and Ramón, like José and Rosa, live in Vista el Valle. Regina participates with her sister Yspírito in the residential *tanda* in the squatters' area of Colonia Paraíso. While consanguineous relationships between Regina and Yspírito are relatively strong, the sisters are divided both by class and by residence. Regina's participation in Yspírito's *tanda* bridges these interstitial gaps. Yspírito's husband Polo, meanwhile, participates in *tapicero* (upholstery) *tandas* with his brother Armando. Within the same residential and class sector, Johnny, Yspírito's son, participates in his sister Norma's *tanda* with the third network of Carenas and Carlotta. Thus a series of links connects Carenas and Carlotta to Johnny and Norma to Yspírito to Regina and then, through Regina's in-laws, to bourgeois Ana. This does not mean that any direct exchanges of information take place among these connections, but, should the need arise, the possibility of mobilizing such connections does exist.

As can be seen from Figure 5.1, five institutional sectors are represented in these networks. Jesús, Ana's husband, is a medical doctor working in the main office of the social security administration, and Petra, Olea's daughter, works in the records office of one of the system's clinics. Elías, Jr. is an office manager in the Treasury Department's tax collector's office, while his sister Rosa works in the Public Works Office. Yspírito's son-in-law and his brother are both employed as policemen in the Transit Police Office. All of these people participate in office *tandas*. As has been suggested, exchange obligations generate normal relations within institutions. Also, however, institutional RCAs make it easier for spouses and relatives to participate in residential RCAs.

As shown in Figure 5.2, both Elías, Jr. and Rosa accumulate money f om their salaries and *tanda* fund shares. Both contribute to their p rents' (Juana and Elías) expenses, and their parents in turn provide money to their parents, José and Rosa. José and Rosa with Olea then contribute money to Ana's bourgeois *tanda*. The fund share from the 40-women bourgeois *tanda* returns via Ana and is distributed to José, Rosa, and Olea.

As I have already suggested, these links to other class and institutional sectors can be mobilized as possible sources of assistance. For example, Carlotta once needed medical assistance, and Carenas asked his *compadre* Johnny for help. Johnny in turn mobilized his network, including his mother Yspírito and his mother's sister, whose husband Ramón is the brother-in-law of Jesús, the medical doctor. Since Carenas could not legitimately acquire medical treatment for Carlotta by means of workmen's benefits, Petra (Olea's daughter and Jesús's and Regina's affinal niece) was called upon to assist in the establishment of a medical record in the documentary section of the local medical clinic where she

Figure 5.2. Circulation of Funds

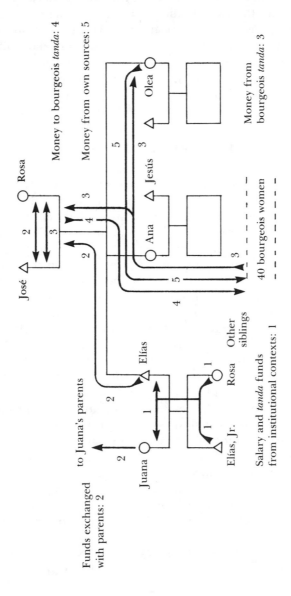

Funds exchanged
with parents: 2

Money to bourgeois *tanda*: 4

Money from own sources: 5

Money from
bourgeois *tanda*: 3

Salary and *tanda* funds
from institutional contexts: 1

worked. That particular clinic did not have the specialized treatment necessary, but by means of the documents acquired through Petra, Carlotta became eligible to receive the best medical treatment in Jesús's main medical office. Petra could not have accomplished this without the collaboration of her fellow office workers with whom she participated in dense network relationships that included a *tanda*, gift giving, and commensality. Thus, while people are divided by a number of cleavages, *tandas* do help to bridge the gaps between them both directly and indirectly.

CULTURAL DIFFUSION

One of the most important consequences of RCAs is that they help diffuse underlying cultural constructs within the Mexican population both in and beyond Mexico. While it is highly likely that for the most part only first-generation Mexicans in the United States participate in such associations, the underlying element of *confianza* will continue to be an important construct in predicting others' behavior, structuring one's behavior with others, and maintaining a reflexive cultural reference to oneself.

In addition, unlike many previous generations of Mexicans migrating to the United States who could count on the security and protection of working-class neighborhoods, for most Mexicans migrating in the present, the uncertainty of the metropolises to which they move selects against the maintenance of social networks, cultural cohesion, and psychological security (Galarza 1981:8–9). Such mobility "delocalizes"[3] the population, and thus the Mexican rotating credit association assists in providing a modicum of security in a very uncertain context, and also in reinforcing the construct of *confianza*. Such a consequence promotes and reestablishes meaning in new contexts. Thus, for Mexicans in the United States in insecure, delocalized urban contexts, the RCA and, equally important, the construct of *confianza* are very significant and adaptive at social, cultural, and individual psychological levels.

DEUTERO-LEARNING: SAVING TO SAVE AND TRUSTING MUTUAL TRUST

Among the most important unintended consequences of RCAs is what Bateson (1978) has termed deutero-learning. He has stated that two types of slopes are expressed in all continuous learning: "The gradient at any point on a simple learning curve . . . we will say chiefly represents rates of proto-learning. If, however, we inflict a series of similar learning experiments on the same subject, we shall find that in each successive experiment the subject has a somewhat steeper proto-learning gradient, that he learns somewhat more rapidly. This progressive change in rate of proto-learning we will call 'deutero-learning'" (167).

To make the idea of deutero-learning clearer, Bateson (166) has likened it to what happens in an experimental setting in which a person "not only solves the problems set him by the experimenter, where each solving is a piece of simple learning; but, more than this, he becomes more and more skilled in the solving of problems." It can be inferred from our data that those saving not only save but, if rewarded, expand the notion of "saving." Not only do people expect mutual trust, but, if rewarded, they expand the expectation of mutual trust. Thus both saving to save and trusting mutual trust are deutero-learned constructs.

Ahorro para ahorrar is deutero-learned in that the habit or custom of saving expands at the moment an act representative of saving occurs or is expected to occur, regardless of the specific context. Participation in RCAs is one such act, as is the saving of the accumulated fund shares.

Confianza en confianza is a deutero-learned construct in that the habit or custom of *confianza* expands at the moment an act representative of trusting will or does occur. Participation in rotating credit associations is one such act, as is the expectation of participating in equivalent actions. *Confianza en confianza* can be considered somewhat more expansive than *ahorro para ahorrar*, since a series of reciprocal modes are expressed in other contexts besides RCAs, as, for example, in commensal, ritual, and socializing activities. Familial, residential, and occupational sectors all select for other reciprocal exchanges besides those involved in the RCAs. Thus, it is likely that a wider deutero-learning process occurs for *confianza* than for saving.

In considering these two deutero-learning constructs in greater detail it should be kept in mind that such details are inferentially derived from both observed behavior and our more formal data. The following descriptions of the details of each construct are validated by the data but are not the data themselves. No single individual would be able to describe such constructs completely, but I infer that such constructs exist from partial statements of informants, from behavior, and from the continuation of the practices themselves. This is a compromise between subconscious cognitive orientations that members of a group may share as equivalencies and a strictly inferential model that represents an abstraction derived from observed behavior. The constructs presented here are neither the predictive model used by others such as Foster (1967) nor a description of a partial world view of those who participate in rotating credit associations.

The central feature of saving to save as a construct is not defined by the intentions or motives of those who enter into the rotating credit association and make the effort to save. Nor are the meanings that are derived from participating in the rotating credit associations by workers, housewives, upper-class women, the elderly, corporate executives, or any others, central to the construct of saving to save. Intention, motivation, and meaning vary with the contexts in which the associations appear. Rather, the essence of saving as an idea is that each person, regardless of context and regardless of intention or meaning derived, has placed his or her contribution in reserve. Saving to save is learned even by the upper-class women who spend their savings lavishly on one of their network members. The fact that these women agree to hold money in reserve until they accumulate enough is a savings activity regardless of intention. Nor does expenditure of the money saved and accumulated define the construct. On the other hand, if the money accumulated is itself further saved, then the savings process is reinforced and expanded. This is the only caveat to the proposition that neither intention nor the specific expenditure contributes to the formation of the construct saving to save.

This construct also extends to the competing administrators as well as the economists in the planning office who hold in reserve a portion of their income; their intention and the unintended consequences do not matter. The core of this proposition is very much like that postulated by Keynesian economics. The simple classical economic assumption about savings states "that savings always flow into investment at the going rate of interest regardless of the level of income" (Klein 1947: 79). Keynes, according to Klein, attacked the assumptions of this assertion and hypothesized that people can make other decisions in regard to what they do with incomes: "They may decide upon saving or consuming their

incomes, and they may decide upon holding idle cash or non-
liquid securities. Each decision requires an economic calculation.
In the former case, individuals decide on the basis of their incomes how much they want to spend on consumption and at the
same time how much they want to save. In the latter case, they
must decide on the basis of alternative rates [of interest] whether
they want to hold their . . . savings in the form of cash or securities" (Klein 1947: 123). Therefore people must decide what to
save out of income for whatever reasons, and they must decide in
what form to hold savings, that is, as money, stocks, bonds, or as
in the present study, as accumulated funds in rotating credit associations. The rate of interest is as variable as the intention to participate but, nevertheless, the decision to set aside money within
such rotating credit associations is an act of saving.

In addition, the specific reward derived from saving is as variable among all sectors as the intention, but that specific reward
probably will influence the *rate* of further expansion of the learned
construct of saving to save. Thus for the upper-class women, prestige rewards emerge from the reciprocal network and the en-
hancement of their positions in that network. But these rewards
do not eliminate the likelihood that for them, too, the learned
construct of saving has expanded. The reward will probably not
increase the rate of learning for them as much as it does for someone who waits 40 months for a Volkswagen, but nevertheless an
expansion process does occur. To deny such a process for upper-
class women would be to deny the concept of deutero-learning or
restrict the process to specific stimuli or rewards. The degree to
which, and how fast, the construct expands is probably linked to
the reliance on saving for meeting culturally constituted goals and
biological necessities. The essence, therefore, of saving to save is
that, regardless of specific intentions or rewards, the construct expands as an unintended consequence as people participate in
rotating credit associations.

Even when people pay fees in *tandas muertas*, learning takes
place, since each saving activity proves rewarding: energy-con-
suming activities are avoided and social exchanges established. At
each rewarded saving activity, an increase in the rate of proto-
learning results. These savings will result in the deutero-learning
of saving as a concept and its expression in behavior, so that saving
to save as a cultural construct expands in use. What seems to be

an uneconomic sort of participation, because it includes the payment of fees, in fact has important learning consequences.

Other elements of the construct saving to save can, however, be inferred from the most frequent uses of the accumulated sums and by extrapolation from the congealed meanings contained in those uses. As will be recalled (see Figure 2.9), saving money was the primary use for money accumulated through the RCAs. This use of accumulated funds shows that the idea of placing something in reserve as a value in itself is not only expansive, but implies an outlook that is directed toward the future. In other words, a delay in the immediate gratification of a perceived need is an inherent aspect of placing something in reserve. The willingness of people engaged in *tandas* or *cundinas* to wait long periods for their fund shares illustrates this willingness to delay gratification of other needs. The very participation in RCAs implies the willingness to postpone the present and wait for the future to provide the means by which to fulfill needs and goals. Such a delay in the gratification of future needs is also apparent in the fact that the most frequent use of saved money is for further saving. Therefore it is suggested that both the participation in RCAs as a saving venture and the use of obtained funds for savings imply an orientation toward the future for the participants, regardless of their intentions or actual expenditures.

Many of the 14 categories of use listed in Figure 2.9 imply outlooks toward the future and planning strategies designed to increase the probability of meeting sociocultural and biological needs. The second most frequent use of funds was to fulfill ritual obligations, which indicates a desire to maintain and generate social relationships in the present and the future on a regularized schedule. A person's future is assured by meeting such obligations since the other person in the exchange is required to provide a gift in return in the future. It is important to note, however, that ritual obligations can also be used to expand existing social networks, and each expansion not only increases the absolute number of social relationships but "social wealth"—the favors and social credits accumulated for future use—as well.

In terms of the strictly material benefits to be derived, each use also implies planning, direction, improvement, and a quest for future as well as present stability. Each material artifact upon which *tanda* or *cundina* funds are to be spent is invested with values.

Money spent on household goods—the third most frequent use—expresses not only "consumer" values but those congealed in the physical presence of the goods. As part of the home, these help to provide a platform for family stability: surrounding familial relationships with physical artifacts reflects the desire to establish, stabilize, and strengthen them. Buying land, investing money, and purchasing a home also indicate a future-oriented outlook aimed at establishing familial or personal security.

That trusting mutual trust is the central construct in most informal and intermediate RCAs in Mexico and in the U.S. Southwest can be inferred from our data. There is no need to review the various graphs and diagrams illustrating the density of *confianza*, or the various mechanisms and processes used to establish it. It is also not necessary to review how the absence of fraud or default is evidence of the profundity of *confianza* between participants, or to review the multiple relationships shown in the ethnodrama and the manner in which *confianza* had become a matter of faith and not discussable.

Yet there are other important elements of *confianza en confianza* that should be discussed. First, the RCA participants were urban dwellers of various classes, either in the United States, where as members of a national minority, they participated in a complex developed social system, or in Mexico where they participated in a "dependent" developing social system. Mexicans south and north of the Rio Grande went about their lives within the structural confines of industrial or industrializing states, segmented by class, sex, age, ethnicity, income, occupation, productive relations, residence, generation, and plural cultural systems. Each segment's content is variously distributed among its constituent populations, so that no single individual ever consistently shares with any other all aspects of each segment. It is probable that each individual develops equivalencies of beliefs and ideas which are appropriate in the same event. Interaction occurs on the basis of equivalencies rather than on that of shared beliefs and ideas of each segment (Wallace 1961). Therefore, even within subsets of groups in urban contexts, the segmented beliefs and ideas of all persons will represent not wholly equivalencies of those beliefs and ideas, but only those portions of those equivalencies that closely "match" in affect, cognition, and evaluation. Those matched equivalencies and not beliefs and ideas themselves then "intersect" (Schwartz 1968: 13). Therefore each interaction is an imperfect one, with only partial equivalencies of beliefs and ideas, represented analytically as cultural "intersects," used as the vehicles for social transactions.

Recognizing that no member of a rotating credit association will have precisely the same qualitative relationship with each of the other members, since in many cases not all members will know each other and since most interaction occurs with only partial equivalencies of beliefs and ideas, people must project trust in mutual trust to those they do not know or with whom qualitative relationships differ. Trust in the association leader is necessary but not sufficient to establish *confianza* in the operational stability of the entire enterprise. All relationships in complex urban societies are segmented and partial, and even the best of dyadic relationships between a rotating credit association leader and member—when, for example, they are husband and wife—is based on partial equivalent beliefs. Therefore it is highly probable that, given the great stress on *confianza* as the single important mediator in social relationships, *confianza en confianza* is an overriding cultural intersect shared by all concerned. It is a kind of lingua franca of Mexican culture used when people entrust their money, energies, needs, and goals to others, or to shape their general expectations toward those they do not know. Because *confianza en confianza* is rewarding, the construct has expanded to become an overriding cultural intersect for most Mexicans.

Confianza en confianza allows persons to have mutual trust in those with whom no social exchange has been cemented. A second important element is that *confianza en confianza* implies trusting in the trustworthiness of self, which makes mutuality possible. It is not accidental that ritual activities have been important in the expenditure of RCA funds. As Erikson (1963: 250) has suggested, "Individual trust must become a common faith, individual mistrust a commonly formulated evil, while the individual's restoration must become part of the ritual practice of many, and must become a sign of trustworthiness in the community." Without a firm sense of personal trustworthiness no such commonality of trust can be expressed in ritual. Mutual trust is trusting not only in the trustworthiness of others but implicitly in the trustworthiness of self. In varying distributions among urban Mexican populations, the trustworthiness of self is an internal construct serving as the basis for potential social intersects.

I use the phrase "trusting in the trustworthiness of self" to distinguish the idea from the usual understanding of "self-trust" as self-reliance, which is probably a form of complex narcissism. Self-trust and self-reliance are indistinguishable in American usage, but self-reliance is not what Erikson means by trust in oneself. He states that what he calls trust coincides with the term confidence, but he prefers the word trust because there is more mutuality implied in the term (1963: 248). "Trusting in the trustworthiness of self" implies that mutuality to a greater degree than either trust or self-trust. Like Erikson with his notion of trust as a general state, I imply in the term "trusting in the trustworthiness of self" the capacity of one's organs to cope with urges and the ability to consider oneself trustworthy enough so that those relying on one will not need to be on guard against possible or probable machinations on one's part.

An enormous literature opposed to this view forms an important part of studies of "national character" done by both Mexicans and non-Mexicans in Mexico. In many Mexican national character studies analysts have concentrated on the most marginal populations as the prism for national characteristics (Hewes 1953–1954; and see especially Lewis 1959, 1961). Mexican psychoanalysts generally support the view of Mexicans as combining characteristics of dependence, distrust, and, as compensation, brutality. Studies ˑy Aramoni (1961), González Pineda (1961), and Ramírez (1959) generally emphasize the men's masking of dependence and weakness by elaborate machismo and distrust of women. The women's lives are basically constructed around the strategy of foiling and passively destroying the male's authority, especially by destroying or in effect castrating their sons and thus the father. From my point of view such studies, while interesting and provocative, basically extrapolate national characteristics from a clinician's Freudian paradigm, in which psychopathology is the object of analysis (see especially Díaz-Guerrero 1951).

Equally inadequate are characterizations of Mexicans in the United States as basically distrustful, defending themselves against the malevolent perceptions of neighbors, and with social and personal distrust as part of social life (De Vos 1975: 36). When the sources for such statements are examined, the striking finding is that they originate in a study of peasants in Tzintzuntzan (Foster 1967) and in a rather dated philosophical interpretation by Octavio Paz (1961). Real doubt should be cast on such generalizations, based as they are on a limited population of peasants in one village and a philosophical treatise interpreting "national character," especially since Paz's characterizations, published in 1950, were based on the alleged effects of the Spanish conquest, 429 years after the event (1521). In addition Madsen (1962) and Rubel (1965) have noted a culturally specific lack of trust in strangers among Mexicans in the United States. On the other hand, empirical research among Chicano schoolchildren (Price-Williams and Ramirez III: 1974) has not verified this assertion.

Both from a theoretical point of view in which culture in complex urban societies is understood in terms of equivalencies and distributions and on empirical grounds, it would seem that to the extent that RCAs and their cultural constructs are pervasive, the gross generalizations proposed by Mexican national character studies and speculations are not very fruitful and probably contribute to unintended stereotypes. Indeed, the opposite conclusions concerning trust among Mexicans in both the United States and Mexico would seem to follow from theoretical considerations and the data generated here.

In summary, two basic elements are characteristic of *confianza en confianza*: first, it is a generalizable construct extended to those with whom no social exchange has been established, and second, it reflects trusting in the trustworthiness of self. Thus it establishes the basis for reciprocal exchange in a variety of class, ethnic, and other contexts. Mexicans will seek out others with whom to have *confianza* because the construct itself, in its various forms and interpretations, functions as a cultural intersect for social interaction and, by providing coherent expectations of others, has positive and adaptive consequences at a deeply psychocultural level. Mutual trust in others eventually reinforces trust in the trustworthiness of self. To trust others who are not known eventually reinforces trust in still others who are yet to be known. Both elements are expansive and increase in scope as long as they are adaptive and rewarded. To deny the learning consequences for such a construct among Mexicans is to deny the validity of learning theory. Whether such constructs do in fact increase and expand is a processual and structural matter, not a motivational one.

6 Conclusions

Previous chapters have discussed the widespread use of rotating credit associations by Mexicans in the United States and Mexico, as well as the various nomenclatures and types developed, their importance, the early development of commercialized associations, and their implications for saving. The symmetry of *tandas vivas* and the congruence between the number of persons, the size of the contribution, the value of the fund share, and the length of the rotational cycle have been discussed, as well as the significance of such congruence.

An examination of the social and cultural contexts in which RCAs were found showed how each context defined categories that served to fix people's relationships and acted as social references. Various methods and boundaries that decrease the risks involved in lending, borrowing, and saving, so that fraud and default are rare, were analyzed. It was suggested that although Mexicans lack the traditional corporate, regional kinship groups found among other U.S. ethnic groups, their participation in binding reciprocal obligations and the statuses generated from and within occupational, familial, and residential networks have equivalent functions. In part, such equivalence is made possible by the density of relations, which are expressed within those networks as natural systems.

Numerous unintended and intended social, political, cultural, and economic consequences derive from the RCAs, and the examples demonstrate that populations are able to adapt to the structural demands of their various contexts. As the ethnodrama demonstrates, however, indeterminacy and tragic failure can arise from the most determined of cultural inventions and constructs, including the RCA and *confianza*. Yet, even the indeterminacy that arises from cultural inventions is selective in the long run, since it pushes Mexicans, like other human populations, beyond their historically and structurally established constructs toward a greater expansion and adaptation of human consciousness.

UNCERTAINTY, INDETERMINACY,
AND RECIPROCITY

A hypothesis was proposed that reciprocal exchange practices like those of the RCAs emerge from a general human condition of indeterminacy and uncertainty. Although reciprocal practices like the RCAs do arise in conditions of "balanced scarcity" (Lomnitz 1977), I have shown that RCAs flourish in other situations as well.

No such balanced scarcity of economic resources was apparent in the political competition between administrators in the bureaucracy described, or among the upper-class women of the Lomas de Chapultepec who used their resources for sumptuous consumption. The networks of elderly bourgeois men and women were, in fact, quite well-off. Among professionals in banking institutions there was no question of balanced scarcity. Nor did it exist among economic forecasters in a central economic planning office in Mexico or among upper-middle-class networks of professionals in Tijuana.

The central features of these domains are not balanced scarcity but indeterminacy and uncertainty. Reciprocal activities like those occurring in rotating credit associations work to reduce perceived uncertainty, in a process analogous to the cognitive-dissonance reduction described by Festinger (1957). Uncertainty in these situations stems from lack of information (Orbach 1979) and makes it impossible to form coherent expectations. Indeterminacy arises in every interpersonal encounter, gaps exist in all human exchanges, and there are limits to how much can be accomplished by innovation and interpretation (Moore 1975: 220). These two elements, then, of indeterminacy and uncertainty, are part of all the contexts reviewed in this work. The marginal populations described here (and by Lomnitz 1977) all face uncertainty and indeterminacy because of economic insecurity. High mobility rates among marginal populations in Los Angeles and extreme economic deprivation in Lomnitz's Cerrada del Condor, as well as in Netzahualcoyótl Izcalli, hamper permanent social relations in spite of people's struggles to establish themselves in dense networks of relations. The middle-class persons living beyond their means are at the brink of cultural boundaries of respectability, clearly an uncertain situation. Women newly separated from their working-class backgrounds and living in new residential and cultural contexts face great uncertainty and social indeterminacy. These women cannot predict whether old needs will be fulfilled by new cultural artifacts and fashion or new needs by old methods of social relations. Among women of all classes uncertainty arises from their partial (as opposed to the more rigid dependence of caste relations) dependence on their husbands. Husbands may or may not be dependable, but this is not the central issue. Rather, for women in most class sectors such dependency relations, like most urban relations, are complex and segmentary, and women are encouraged to establish independent domains. In their sumptuous gift-giving, upper-class women are celebrating their independent domain and their success at "pulling it off," often without their husbands' awareness.

Certainly occupational and institutional contexts usually create uncertainty because of the single-stranded goals of most enterprises, private or public. Indeterminate social relations are always a part of institutional sectors, especially where survival depends on the participants' politics, as illustrated in the discussion of RCAs among administrators. Political competition itself creates greater gaps between competitors and even further segmentation of relationships. Everyone may know that there are rules for political competition, but the rules are always imperfectly shared. Competitors work more from signals than from meaning.

Familial *tandas* with multiple relations are not guarantees against unpredictable abuses, as the ethnodrama illustrates. Uncertainty and indeterminacy can arise where least expected because the understandings between people can be so certain and fixed that they become matters of faith which are not discussable. Like religious beliefs whose precepts are not open to question or discussion, intense relationships generate congruent understandings whose discussion is a breach of faith.

Personal uncertainty for individuals can also be created by dynamic social processes like population mobility. Thus the shift within RCAs from no fees to fees may emerge not because of "learned" economic rational strategies but as adaptations to indeterminacy and uncertainty created by population mobility. Even beyond social processes, the end of the life cycle for the Mexican elderly creates great uncertainty: although it is certain that life will end, when it will do so is unknown. That quality of uncertainty and the certain rupturing of social bonds underlie the elderly's deep commitment to recreation and to setting up future obligations.

The crucial point is that the balanced scarcity hypothesis limits our ability to explain the rise of such a widespread reciprocal practice as the rotating credit association. In some settings the balanced scarcity notion may be important to the rise of reciprocity as a central exchange mode within the rotating credit association. But practices in which the central exchange mode is reciprocity emerge more generally from uncertainty generated by context, indeterminate social relations, dynamic social processes, and the life cycle. Reciprocity is a statement of the attempt to establish a social relationship on an enduring basis. Whether symmetrical or asymmetrical, the exchange expresses and symbolizes human social interdependence.

But like all human systems, including reciprocal exchange, rotating credit associations are mutable so that in fact to establish such a system is to admit its mutability (Moore 1975: 221). This is a human, not a Mexican, condition. Like all humans, Mexicans call on inventive practices to establish interdependence based on *confianza* in spite of the fact that the very process of invention and invocation establishes its own mutability. All such mutable practices are attempts to "fix" and regularize action and persons in the face of uncertainty and indeterminacy.

FIXITY, REGULARIZATION, AND UNIONS OF TRUST

All the data presented in relation to the boundaries and safeguards surrounding reciprocal exchange relations established via the rotating credit associations point to attempts by the Mexican populations—like all human populations—to "fix" and "regularize" actions and persons in predictable sequences in order to form coherent expectations. As the data have shown, organizers and participants in the RCAs have developed rules, boundaries, rituals, and overall cultural constructs of *confianza*. These help reduce the effects of uncertainty and assist in placing persons in fixed and determined statuses and relationships. Thus, organizers use *confianza* to establish the identity and worth of prospective RCA members. The intense gift giving and commensal activities of female office employees are regularizing actions which place both new and old personnel in predictable patterns. The ritualization of "passing on" an RCA leadership through visits, commensal activities, and a special supper is a repetitive means not only to secure a new leader but to reduce the uncertainty created by a change in leadership. As Moore (1975: 221) has pointed out in relation to all symbolic repetitions, "They represent stability and continuity acted out and re-enacted: visible continuity."

Ethnic boundaries established to keep others out, like those created by Mexicans in the southwestern United States, are also part of regularization. The fact that most RCAs restricted members to other Mexicans or equivalent cultural groups supports this. Occupational and class distinctions were used to establish eligibility and reduce uncertainty in institutional and occupational contexts. Certainly the elite workers of the Veracruz oil fields accomplished this by admitting only those with seniority.

In the network of *tanda* participants in Monterrey (Figure 5.1), Ana as a new member of the bourgeoisie cemented her social existence by reference to the past through the incorporation of her working-class mother's and sister's contributions. Each political signal between administrators stimulated competition, but the RCAs regularly identified who was on the outs with whom, thus reducing uncertainty for all competitors. For the elderly Mexicans, *tandas* are attempted regularizations of the most poignant sort, for they are dissolved at the end of the life cycle, which is the final regularity. Thus, in all these contexts, the processes, structures, and exchange relations as well as the cultural constructs making up the rotating credit associations as unions of trust serve to reduce uncertainty and counter the indeterminacy of social living.

Like all cultural beings, Mexicans who have used inventive practices generate deep underlying cultural constructs to reduce anxiety and prove their chances of survival by adaptation. Both the practice of the rotating credit association and the intersects used probably promote well-being and survival. Needless to say, different populations will develop different practices, intersects, and constructs. Among Anglo-Americans in the United States, individualism rather than mutual trust has generated a heavy reliance on large-scale institutional forms rather than intense, multiple networks. Regardless of what constructs, intersects, or practices are used by a population, they must remain flexible and potentially positive for that population. Just as important, populations using such human inventions as the rotating credit associations and allied constructs must be flexible enough to discard them. Mexicans are little different from other human beings in this regard, so that when *confianza en confianza, ahorro para ahorrar, tandas,* and *cundinas,* and all other such reciprocating forms and constructs cease to be useful and positively adaptive, they too will be discarded or changed. Such is the human experience and the Mexican experience.

Appendix A: Six-Person, 30-Week Tanda

Person	Turns	Contribution	Weekly Total	Weeks	Total Paid Out	Total Received	
1	1–10	100	1,000	11–30	20,000	20,000	5,000 from person 2 (500 weekly for 10 weeks) 5,000 from person 3 (500 weekly for 10 weeks) 5,000 from person 4 (500 weekly for 10 weeks) 4,000 from person 5 (400 weekly for 10 weeks) 1,000 from person 6 (100 weekly for 10 weeks)
2	11–15	100	500	1–10 16–30	12,500	12,500	5,000 from person 1 (1,000 weekly for 5 weeks) 2,500 from person 3 (500 weekly for 5 weeks) 2,500 from person 4 (500 weekly for 5 weeks) 2,000 from person 5 (400 weekly for 5 weeks) 500 from person 6 (100 weekly for 5 weeks)
3	16–20	100	500	1–15 21–30	12,500	12,500	5,000 from person 1 (1,000 weekly for 5 weeks) 2,500 from person 2 (500 weekly for 5 weeks) 2,500 from person 4 (500 weekly for 5 weeks) 2,000 from person 5 (400 weekly for 5 weeks) 500 from person 6 (100 weekly for 5 weeks)
4	21–25	100	500	1–20 26–30	12,500	12,500	5,000 from person 1 (1,000 weekly for 5 weeks) 2,500 from person 2 (500 weekly for 5 weeks) 2,500 from person 3 (500 weekly for 5 weeks) 2,000 from person 5 (400 weekly for 5 weeks) 500 from person 6 (100 weekly for 5 weeks)
5	26–29	100	400	1–25 and 30	10,400	10,400	4,000 from person 1 (1,000 weekly for 4 weeks) 2,000 from person 2 (500 weekly for 4 weeks) 2,000 from person 3 (500 weekly for 4 weeks) 2,000 from person 4 (500 weekly for 4 weeks) 400 from person 6 (100 weekly for 4 weeks)
6	30	100	100	1–29	2,900	2,900	1,000 from person 1 (1,000 weekly for 1 week) 500 from person 2 (500 weekly for 1 week) 500 from person 3 (500 weekly for 1 week) 500 from person 4 (500 weekly for 1 week) 400 from person 5 (400 weekly for 1 week)

Appendix B:
Contract of Agreement

20,000 [50,000; 100,000; 150,000] PESO *MUTUALISTA*

He quedado enterado de la existencia de una Asociación Civil con fines mutualistas con las siguientes caracteristicas:

DENOMINACION: Mutualista de Yucatán (pseudonym)

Domicilio: Mérida, Yuc.

Objeto: formar fondos de ahorro de $20,000.00, [50,000: $50,000.00; 100,000: $100,000.00; 150,000: $150,000.00] para cada uno de los Asociados que les permita adquirir o reconstruir bienes immuebles o y constituir gravámenes sobre ellos, y formar fondos de defunción e invalidez total permanente, por la misma cantidad, para el caso de fallecimiento o invalidez de un asociado.

Número de accíones: 40. [50,000: 50; 100,000: 50; 150,000: 50]

Valor de cada acción: $20,000.00, [50,000: $50,000.00; 100,000: $100,000.00; 150,000: $150,000.00] que es el importe del fondo de ahorro.

Duración: 327 [50,000: 394; 100,000: 394; 150,000: "393 semanas y cuoto complementaria de $162.00."] semanas.

Régimen legal: Código Civil del Estado de Yucatán y leyes relativas.

Obligaciones para formar los fondos de ahorro.

I.—Contribuir con 327 [50,000: 394; 100,000: "—Todos los Asociados pagarán la cantidad de $212 semanales antes de resultar beneficiado con el fondo de ahorro"; 150,000: 393] aportaciones semanales de $54.00 [50,000: $106.00; 150,000: $320,00] cada uno.

II.—Contribuir con aportaciones semanales de $26.00 [50,000: $64.00; 150,000: $190.00] además de las anteriores, a partir de la fecha en que le corresponda al asociado recibir el fondo de ahorro, y ahorro, y durante el resto de duracion del plan de ahorro, o sean $80.000 [50,000: $170.000; 150,000: $510.000] semanales.

[100,000: "—Todos los Asociados pagarán la cantidad de $340 semanales a partir de la fecha en que les corresponda recivir el fondo de ahorro."]

III.—Contribuir para formar los fondos de defunción o invalidez, a prorrata junto con los demás asociados con la parte proporcional que le corresponde de las cuotas faltantes del asociado o asociados fallecidos o invalidados.

[100,000: "—Todos los Asociados contribuirán a prorrata con la parte proporcional que le corresponde le las cuotas faltantes del asociado o asociados fallecidos o invalidados."]

IV.—Gastos: de estas cuotas se destinarán el 6% en las sencillas y el 8% en las premiadas para las siguientes erogacio nes: Cobranzas y Administración (pago a cobradores, local, luz, teléfono, Contador Fiscal, Contador Privado, papelería y honorarios de los Directivos).

Fondos de defunción: $20,000.00. [50,000: $50,000.00; 100,000: $100,000.00; 150,000: $20,000.00]

Edad límite: de 15 a 60 años. Período de espera para que funcione el seguro: un año. [100,000: ". . . a partir del primer serteo."]

Seguro de invalidez total permanente: los coasociados cubrirán la cuota sencilla del accidentado o invalidado.

Asambleas iniciales cada diez semanas.

Quedó enterado asimismo de los presentes, después de dejar constituida la Asociación acordaron designar su Junta Directiva, la cual quedó constituida de la siguiente manera:

PRESIDENTE:

SECRETARIO:

TESORERO:

Enterado de todo lo anterior solicito que se me acepte como asociado, con todos sus derechos y obligaciones.

En espera de la respuesta favorable, acompaño a la presente solicitud, la cantidad de $50.00 [50,000: $75.00; 100,000: $150; 150,000: $200.00] para cubrir la parte proporcional que me corresponde en los gastos de organización legal de la Asociación y me es grato suscribirme como

Su atto. y S. S.

Fecha ——————————————

Nombre—————————————— Tel. Of. ——————————

Dirección—————————————— Tel. ——————————

Dirección para el cobro: ——————————————————

Días y forma de cobro: ——————————————————

El que premia primero, paga $26,000.00 [50,000: $66,340.00; 100,000: $132,680; 150,000: $198,692.00]

El que premia de último, paga $17,062.50 [50,000: $41,764.50; 100,000: $83,529; 150,000: $125,922.00]

. . . .

Recibí del Sr. (a) ——————————————————————

la cantidad de $50.00 [50,000: $75.00; 100,000: *drops all wording but* "$150.00 M.N."; 150,000: $200.00] (Cincuenta pesos 00/100 M. N.)

en concepto de Cuota de Inscripción del Grupo ——————————

de Mutualistas de Yucatán, A. C., quien se compromete a cumplir con los Estatutos de la Sociedad.

Mérida, Yuc.,——————————de 197————

DIRECTOR-TESORERO,

Lic.

Notes

INTRODUCTION

1. I usually use the term "Mexican" for persons residing in either Mexico or the United States. Although "Chicano" is used for those born in the United States of Mexican heritage, Mexican is the generally preferred term.

2. These constructs are deutero-learned. Learning to trust has an expansive dimension, so that one act of trust sets the construct for greater trust without their needing to have been any previous acts of trust. Thus *confianza* is described here as a cultural construct that is both expansive and generalizable.

CHAPTER 1

1. Camilo Garcia Parra, my research assistant in 1978–1979, was responsible for the collection of portions of these data as well as for the initial design of the questionnaire. Scholars interested in seeing the questionnaire should write to the author.

2. Peter Blau (1964) has made the distinction between "social exchange" and strictly "economic exchange." He states that the former differs in important ways from the latter in that it is a nonspecific favor in which there is a general expectation of some future return whose exact nature is not stipulated in advance. An economic exchange, on the other hand, is an obligation that is specifically defined and is agreed to at the time the transaction takes place. Social exchange also differs significantly in that it generates feelings of "personal obligation, gratitude, and trust; purely economic exchange as such does not" (94). In addition, Blau says that social exchanges do not have an exact price "in terms of a single quantitative medium of exchange" and that this is a substantive fact (94–95). The problem with Blau's assertions lies in his use of definitional constructs such as "strictly economic exchange" and "purely economic exchange," two definitional requirements seldom found, even in the most capitalistic of market exchanges. Even in across-the-counter transactions, there has to be a diffusive quality attached to the medium of exchange ("In God We Trust" is printed on all American currency and an all-seeing eye appears on dollar bills), to the clerk who will guarantee the fairness

of the exchange, to the person on whom one relies to provide information on the quality of the product, and to the product itself. Few transactions can really be understood to be "strictly" or "purely" economic exchanges, without any diffusive qualities at all. I would assert that cultural values within the transactions as well as the contexts in which transactions occur will define the transaction.

3. Katzin (1959: 440) has stated that Bernice Kaplan reported RCAs among Peruvian Indians, but I have been unable to find verification of this claim in the literature. However, Reymundo Paredes, a Peruvian anthropologist, has confirmed their existence among middle-class persons in Lima. They are termed *"panderos"* and usually operate among family members or friends. In addition, he described the *pandero techo* (literally roof association), which rotates homes, as well as *panderos* of cars rotated by Volkswagen automobile agencies. These last are analogous to the Mexican *tandas de casas* and *tandas de Volkswagen*. Paredas stated that the automobile *panderos* are advertised in Lima newspapers (personal communication, July 31, 1980). *Panderos* have also been reported in Brazil and Panama (de Wolfe 1982).

4. In 1972, Thomas Weaver of the University of Arizona first suggested a possible relationship between the Chinese *hui* and the Mexican *tandas*. He said that one of his students had uncovered *hui* among Chinese benevolent associations in Tucson, Arizona.

5. During the period that Plutarco Calles served as president of Mexico (1924–1928) and later, when he was the power behind the throne (1929–1935), Chinese were expelled from most of Mexico so that Chinese immigrants settled permanently in only a few areas.

6. See Wu (1974) for a description of the *hui* in New Guinea, Light (1972) for those in the United States, and Broady (1958) for those in Great Britain.

7. Voluntary cooperative associations, in which *tanda*-like structures were formed for different purposes, have, however, been numerous in Arizona, Colorado, and New Mexico. For example, in New Mexico in the copper town of Hurley, Chicano miners in the 1920s formed cooperatives (Liga Obrera Mexicana) based on *confianza* in which 40 or more miners and their families pooled relatively large amounts of money on a weekly basis. The money was used to open and maintain cooperative stores outside of the company town of Hurley. Miners and their families thus circumvented the necessity of buying overpriced items in the company store, much as Mexicans today circumvent interest charges by forming *tandas* of Volkswagens and Datsuns. The history of the formation of voluntary associations by Mexicans north and south of the Rio Bravo is a rich one.

8. See *La Revista de Mérida*, February 9, 1900, p. 3; June 12, 1902, p. 6; and February 25, 1908, p. 3. The February 9, 1900, article which is entitled "*Caja de Ahorros Monte Piedad de Yucatán Sociedad Coperativa*," announced the formation of a 100,000-peso fund which was to continue the first fund established in June 1898. Each contribution was worth 100

pesos with protective beneficiary privileges for *socios* (members); a deduction was made to cover expenses. Each participant was provided with a legal title of association. From this description, it is clear the *mutualistas* at least antedate the 20th-century, nor do their operations appear to have changed very much (see Chapter 2).

CHAPTER 2

1. Inflation in Mexico has increased steadily since 1973. In 1973 the national retail price index rose by 12.2 percent. In 1974 wholesale prices rose by 21.9 percent and consumer prices by 23.7 percent. In the fiscal year ending March 1978, consumer prices rose by 17.5 percent (*Quarterly Economic Review of Mexico* 1979: 20).

2. See Chapter 4, and Vélez-Ibañez 1978a for an explanation of the concept of "ethnodrama."

CHAPTER 3

1. The term "Hispanic" is used rather than Mexican because in most of the theater chains there are both managers who participate in the RCAs and members who are from Peru, Guatemala, and other Latin American countries. The great majority of both managers and employees are in fact Mexicans.

2. Projectionists seem to form their own RCAs across the theater chains because of their exclusive union status and skill. The rest of the associations are in the hands of the cashiers.

3. Light did not include any Mexican material in his work probably because no published materials were available at the time he carried out his study. It would be interesting to see how he might have explained the presence of the *cundinas* or *tandas* in the U.S. Southwest; these are without the corporate structures he seemed to have thought were important for the development of the Chinese and Japanese RCAs.

CHAPTER 4

1. Wallace (1961) is the seminal work in the development of the idea that people interact in events without having the *same* organized beliefs or values or ideas. The implication is that in fact culture is "distributed," not shared, and this distribution selects for greater expansion and adaptation of human consciousness beyond the limits of any individual at any point in history.

2. The structural and historical patterns of Netzahualcoyótl as well as

the ecological characteristics of the area are déscribed in Vélez-Ibañez (1978a: 269–270) in the following manner:

"STRUCTURAL CHARACTERISTICS. Located in the eastern part of the state of Mexico and 17 kilometers from the center of Mexico City but northeast of the Federal District, Ciudad Netzahualcoyótl Izcalli (The Place Where Hungry Coyote Resides, from the Nahuatl) is one of a number of sprawling cities growing around the city of Mexico and the Federal District. The area, now comprising 62 square kilometers of the former lakebed of Texcoco is populated by over a million persons largely from two sources of migration: first, skilled and semiskilled persons, products of federal policies designed to favor those who can afford the relatively high rents in the Federal District; and second, the stream of migrants composed of the rural and urban unemployed, the chronically underemployed, and the busca chambas (work seekers) for whom Netzahualcoyótl represents a region of possibilities.

As a locality, Netzahualcoyótl is dependent on nonlocal wage sources; on nonlocal transportation systems; on nonlocal materials, foodstuffs, and manufactured consumer goods; on nonlocal markets for local sweatshop-produced goods; on nonlocal nationally appointed state and federal officials serving at the municipal level; on nonlocal state and nation-directed planning, service, judicial, and educational institutions, and on referent values and beliefs communicated and reinforced through mass entertainment networks. Such structural characteristics result in the establishment of a resource-drained, nonproductive locality in which a large supply of cheap or nonpaid labor is present for the exclusive use of public or private supralocal interests in Mexico City.

In large measure exploited within and without the locality, surrounded by fetid wastes dumped from the sewer canals from Mexico City, sickened by contaminated water sources and polluted air, the heterogeneous population of a million plus, nevertheless, survives in relative good order with extended bonds of friendship, kinship, and communal assistance. These bonds, reinforced in revolving credit associations, life cycle rituals, commensal activities, visitations, and self-help projects (constantly tested by the many supralocal intersections which exact great strains on these relationships), are the basis of the many moral circles of multiple relations which make up the locality *in toto.*

ECOLOGICAL AND DEMOGRAPHIC CHARACTERISTICS. Netzahual-coyótl is an ecological nightmare from which 200,000 persons commute daily to seek work, work intermittently, or (for the fortunate 25% or so who are steadily employed) to reach their place of employment (Vélez-Ibañez 1977). Resting on soil of saltpeter, the locality is plagued with rain and sandstorms which sweep through during both the wet and dry seasons. To the east is a large open expanse of plain between the locality and the municipality of Chimalhuacán, located three kilometers away. No natural or man-made objects interfere with the sandstorms from this plain nor from the lakebed north of the city. This lakebed parallels the locality for 95 blocks and sewage spills into it from five drainage pipes. This creates a most unhealthy environment. Nauseous fumes permeate the air and in the dry season, fecal particles are ingested by the inhabitants. In addition, in the wet season, mounds of collected mud and refuse blown in from the lake pile up like modern obscene pyramids from which, occasionally, pepenadores (garbage pickers) collect their goods to sell, and on which children jump and play.

Such an ecological imbalance combines with acute overpopulation to produce an unfavorable social climate for family stability and physical and psychological health. With an increase of 10,000 persons per month culminating in an estimated population of over two million by 1980, present median family sizes of 7.6 will be maintained, fecundity rates for women between ages 25 and 50 will not decrease until the sixth child, the surplus population of children (56,000 between ages 6 and 14) who cannot enter educational facilities because of limited space will not be reduced, and the death rate for children ages 0–4 (75% in one of the neighborhoods) will continue. Such characteristics are aggravated by a combined family median income of less than $80 a month for 65% of the families in this locality. With such economic strain, it is little wonder that over 81% of the population live in dwellings that have three rooms or less."

CHAPTER 5

1. See Anderson 1966; Anderson and Anderson 1958; Banton 1956, 1957; Baskuaskas 1971; Brandel-Srier 1971; Comhaire 1950; Dotson 1965; Doughty 1969, 1970; Frankenberg 1957; Freedman 1967; Green 1969; Hamer 1967; Handleman 1967; Hausknecht 1962; Hogg 1965; Kapferer 1969; Kenny 1961, 1962; Leeds 1965; Levine 1965; Little 1965, 1967, 1971; Mangin 1965; Meillasoux 1968; Noble 1970; Norbeck 1966; Parkin 1966; Skinner 1974; Soen and de Camaramond 1972; Treudley 1966; Wallerstein 1966; and Wheeldon 1969. In addition, there is a vast literature on such adaptive strategies as voluntary associations. Cohen's excellent book (1974) is a case in point.

2. Polanyi (1957) and Dalton (1968) have suggested that the basic notions of economics like maximization, which assumes that individuals will make decisions rationally in order to achieve the maximum reward, should only be used for systems of market exchange. Other systems organize exchange not on the basis of market maximization of scarce goods but on what both authors regard as different modes of exchange like reciprocity or redistribution. It is therefore inappropriate to describe qualitatively different social institutions in terms based on market exchange. Polanyi's and Dalton's position is called the *substantivist* position; it argues that economic systems should be compared according to the mode by which the means of subsistence are organized and exchanged.

The *formalist* position denies the validity of this approach and suggests that all economic systems can be fruitfully analyzed by the models of formal economics. Neither of the two approaches is quite acceptable to those espousing more radical approaches.

3. Delocalization is the process by which adaptive cultural systems are uprooted from their urban and rural contexts by structural and ecological changes. An area becomes "localized" once a population establishes meaningful patterns of social relations that assist in meeting the biocultural needs and goals of the population. I have developed this concept in relation to elderly Mexicans living in other circumstances in the United States (see Vélez-Ibañez, Verdugo, and Nuñez 1981).

Glossary

ahorro *(saving)*   Any form of saving activity

ahorro para ahorrar *(saving to save)*   The deutero-learned construct inferred from these data. The construct expands regardless of intent and use as long as rewards of some sort are generated. The construct includes future planning, goal orientations of stability, delayed gratification, and an interest in future generations.

amistad *(friendship)*   One of the relationships of reciprocity important in maintaining dense "fixed" relations

asesor *(consultant-broker)*   An individual who serves interstitial functions at different levels within many Mexican institutional sectors. Sometimes a broker, sometimes a confidant, and with or without portfolio, the *asesor* is necessary to many economic and political transactions. The term has an essentially positive connotation.

bolita *(little ball)*   One of the terms used to designate a rotating credit association. The name is probably derived from the numbered balls in wire hoppers used in lotteries.

cacique *(political leader)*   The traditional view of *caciquismo* is that it is an informal political method of control by a small association of individuals under one leader (Friedrich 1965: 190). Violence, verbal persuasion, and the use of collateral relatives are the principal methods of political control. It is also considered a transitional urban phenomenon restricted to evolving low-income settlements (Cornelius 1973: 150). I find that such leadership is neither specific to low-income areas nor transitory (Vélez-Ibañez 1978a).

caja de ahorros *(a box of savings)*   Informal and formal credit unions, which are widely distributed throughout Mexico

chingar *(to screw)*   The emic descriptor for exploitation, marginality, powerlessness, or the cause of disrupted social relationships. It is equivalent to the Anglo-Saxon "fuck." In its noun form the word refers to a powerful individual. Some literature has used this emic descriptor to characterize the Mexican personality, motivation, and relationships.

compadrazgo *(cogodparenthood)*   An important Mexican fictive relationship that is ceremonially sanctioned and provides the impetus for network expansion in various contexts

confianza *(mutual trust)* The Mexican cultural construct indicating the willingness to engage in generalized reciprocity. It may be open, processual, or closed.

confianza en confianza *(trusting mutual trust)* The deutero-learned construct inferred from these data. The construct expands as long as reciprocity and exchange relations are maintained. The construct ultimately implies trust in the trustworthiness of self since mutual trust as an organizing intersect for social relations cannot be used without a sense of trust in the ability to cope with one's organs.

coyote *(consultant-broker)* An intermediary but with a more negative connotation than the *asesor*, and carrying an implication that illegal or unethical activities are being negotiated

cuates *(pals)* Two or more intimate male friends

cuchuval *(to raise a reunion)* A Guatemalan variant of the rotating credit association, from the Quichee

cundina (from the verb *cundir*, to spread) One of the terms used to designate a rotating credit association, the second most frequently used by our informants. It is found primarily in northern Mexico and the southwestern United States.

cundinero A person who organizes rotating credit associations on a part-time or full-time basis

ethnodrama A method of exposition of data couched within a reconstruction of events as like their unfolding as possible. Actors, roles, decisions, and cultural and structural constraints are emphasized. Such a technique is very much a part of situational urban analysis.

fictive friendship An interpersonal relationship in which the idiom of describing the relationship is "friendship" but in which the relationship is specific only to such contexts as clubs, institutions, and periodic events. Such friendships lack density, continuous reciprocity, and committed affect. Such relationships are more probable among urban peoples for whom mobility and flexibility are required as a consequence of complex wage structures. Academics, for example, because of the congruence between vertical and horizontal mobility, participate in such fictive friendship networks. Status changes which are frequent among academics require geographical movement in many instances. Fictive friendships serve a variety of social, affective, and professional needs, but are marked by their ease of transferability across institutions. See especially S. F. Moore (1978) for the seminal discussion of the term and the proper context for its use.

flechazos *(arrows)* Verbal barbs used as a means of reducing someone's social prestige

first turn The first turn may be the reserve asked by a specialist in order to ensure the timely distribution of the fund share. The turn may also, however, be provided to the organizer as a favor in return for organizing the association, but in this case it is not free.

free first turn The free first turn is the fee charged by a specialist and does not obligate the organizer to contribute to the association. Also known as *el cero* and first turn

fuerte–pequeña *(strong–tiny)* The former term refers to long-standing rotating credit associations, involving larger sums and more members than the latter.

fund share The amount actually rotated to members of a rotating credit association

gente de rancho *(people from ranches)* The urban designation for rural persons, with a pejorative connotation of "country bumpkins"

hui *(association)* The Chinese version of the rotating credit association

Liga Obrera Mexicana *(Mexican Worker's League)* A mutual aid society composed of Chicano miners in Hurley, New Mexico in the early 1920s

maquiladoras Labor-intensive light industry, sometimes used to describe sweatshops

muerta–viva *(dead–alive)* The former are rotating credit associations in which a specialist charges a fee, free first turn, zero, or a percentage. The latter involve no market relations and are therefore convivial and reciprocal.

mutualista One of the terms used to designate a rotating credit association. Designating both informally and formally organized types, the term is used only in Yucatán.

padrino politico *(political godfather)* A type of fictive friendship in which a person of influence becomes sponsor and protector for another seeking to enter institutional contexts in private, public, and labor sectors. While ritual relations generated through *compadrazgo* (cogodparenthood) may also bind the relationship between the *padrino politico* and those being sponsored, it is nevertheless often a single-interest and always a dominant-subordinate relationship.

pandero (perhaps a *bulge*) The Peruvian version practiced in Lima. Other types include *pandero techo* (roof associations) and automobile *panderos*.

paracaidista *(parachutist)* Land squatters

polla *(pool, as in card games)* An RCA fund or the participants in an RCA

pretenciosa(o) *(pretentious)* The term used by working-class women for middle-class persons

quincela (derivative of *quincena*, fortnight) One of the terms used to designate a rotating credit association

quiniela *(betting pool)* One of the terms used to designate a rotating credit association

regalos *(gifts)* A reciprocal exchange of gifts forming part of the tripartite exchange system of rotating credit association, commensality, and gifts among women in various institutional contexts

rifa *(raffle)* One of the terms used to designate a rotating credit association

rol *(roll)* One of the terms used to designate a rotating credit association

ronda *(round)* One of the terms used to designate a rotating credit association

socio *(member)* The term used for members of *mutualistas*, also used in some of the *tandas* of Veracruz

tanda *(turn)* One of the terms used to designate a rotating credit association, the one found most often in this research

una union de confianza *(a bond of mutual trust)* An emic definition of the rotating credit association

vaca *(cow)* One of the terms used to designate a rotating credit association

vaquita *(calf)* One of the terms used to designate a rotating credit association

zero turn The fee charged by a specialist, also known as *el cero* or free first turn

Bibliography

ADAMS, RICHARD N.
  1975 *Energy and Structure, A Theory of Social Power.* Austin: University of Texas Press.
ADEYEYE, S. O.
  1981 The Place of "Esusu Clubs" in the Development of the Co-operative Movement in Nigeria. Symposium on Traditional Co-operation and Social Organization and Enterprise. Intercongress of the International Union of Anthropological and Ethnological Sciences, Amsterdam.
ANDERSON, R. T.
  1966 Rotating Credit Associations in India. *Economic Development and Cultural Change* 14:334–339.
ANDERSON, ROBERT T., AND GALLATIN ANDERSON
  1958 Voluntary Associations and Urbanization. *American Journal of Sociology* 65:265–273.
ARAMONI, ANICETO
  1961 *Psicoanalisis de la Dinamica de un Pueblo.* Mexico, D.F.: UNAM.
ARDENER, SHIRLEY
  1964 The Comparative Study of Rotating Credit Associations. *Journal of the Royal Anthropological Institute* 94:201–209.
ASIWAJU, A. I.
  1979 Colonial Approach to Rural Co-operative Production in West Africa, 1910–1960. University of Lagos Central Research Committee.
BAILEY, F. G.
  1969 *Stratagems and Spoils: A Social Anthropology of Politics.* New York: Schocken Books.
  1971 *Gifts and Poison: The Politics of Reputation.* New York: Schocken Books.
BANTON, MICHAEL
  1956 Adaptation and Integration in the Social System of Temne Immigrants in Freetown. *Africa* 26:354–368.
  1957 *West African City: A Study of Tribal Life in Freetown.* London: Oxford University Press.
BASKAUSKAS, LUICIJA
  1971 An Urban Enclave: Lithuanian Refugees in Los Angeles. Ph.D. dissertation, University of California at Los Angeles.

BATESON, GREGORY
1978 *Steps to an Ecology of Mind.* New York: Ballantine Books.
BLAU, PETER
1964 *Exchange and Power in Social Life.* New York: John Wiley and Sons.
BLOK, ANTON
1974 *The Mafia of a Sicilian Village, 1860–1960.* New York: Harper and Row.
BOISSEVAIN, JEREMY
1974 *Friends of Friends: Networks, Manipulators and Coalitions.* New York: St. Martin's Press.
BONNETT, AUBREY W.
1976 Rotating Credit Associations among Black West Indian Immigrants in Brooklyn: An Exploratory Study. Ph.D. dissertation, City University of New York.
DE BOURBOURG, BRASSEUR
1862 *Gramatica de la Lengua Quichee.* Paris: Auguste Duran, Libraire.
BRANDEL-SRIER, MIA
1971 *Reeftown Elite: A Study of Social Mobility in a Modern African Community on the Reef.* London: Routledge and Kegan Paul.
BROADY, MAURICE
1958 The Chinese in Great Britain. In Morton H. Fried, ed., *Colloquium on Overseas Chinese.* New York: Institute of Pacific Relations.
CARLOS, MANUEL L.
1973 Fictive Kinship and Modernization in Mexico: A Comparative Analysis. *Anthropological Quarterly* 46:75–91.
CARLOS, MANUEL L., AND BO ANDERSON
1981 Political Brokerage and Network Politics in Mexico: The Case of a Representative Dominance System. In David Miller and Bo Anderson, eds., *Networks, Exchange, and Coercion: The Elementary Theory and Its Applications.* New York: Elsevier.
CHANG, CHING CHIEH
1956 The Chinese in Latin America: A Preliminary Geographical Survey with Special Reference to Cuba and Jamaica. Ph.D. dissertation, University of Maryland.
COHEN, ABNER
1974 *Urban Ethnicity.* London: Tavistock.
COMHAIRE, SYLVIA
1950 Associations on the Basis of Origin in Lagos, Nigeria. *American Catholic Sociological Review* 11:234–236.
COPE, THOMAS, AND DONALD V. KURTZ
1980 Default and the Tanda: A Model Regarding Recruitment for Rotating Credit Associations. *Ethnology* 19:213–231.
CORNELIUS, WAYNE
1973 Political Learning among the Urban Poor: The Impact of Resi-

dential Context. *Sage Professional Papers. Comparative Political Series.* Beverly Hills, Calif.: Sage Publications.

DALTON, GEORGE
  1968 Introduction. In George Dalton, ed. *Primitive Archaic, and Modern Economics: Essays of Karl Polanyi.* Garden City, N.Y.: Doubleday/Anchor.

DE VOS, GEORGE
  1975 Ethnic Pluralism: Conflict and Accommodation. In George De Vos and Lola Romanucci-Ross, eds., *Ethnic Identity: Cultural Continuities and Change.* Palo Alto, Calif.: Mayfield Publishing Company.

DE WOLFE, EVELYN
  1982 Fund Pools Blocked by Postal Law. *Los Angeles Times,* February 21.

DÍAZ-GUERRERO, ROGELIO
  1951 *Estudios de Psicología del Mexicano.* Mexico, D.F.: Ed. Porrua y Obregon.

DOTSON, FLOYD
  1965 A Note on Participation in Voluntary Associations in a Mexican City. In *Readings in Contemporary Latin American Culture.* New York: Selected Academic Readings.

DOUGHTY, PAUL L.
  1969 La Cultura de Regionalismo en la Vida de Lima, Peru. *America Indigena* 29:949–981.
  1970 Behind the Back of the City: "Provincial" Life in Lima, Peru. In William Mangin, ed., *Peasants and Cities: Readings in the Anthropology of Urbanization.* Boston: Houghton Mifflin Co.

EMBREE, J. F.
  1939 *Suye Mura: A Japanese Village.* Chicago: University of Chicago Press.

ERIKSON, ERIK H.
  1963 *Childhood and Society.* 2d ed. New York: W. W. Norton & Co.

FALLERS, LLOYD
  1965 *Bantu Bureaucracy: A Century of Political Evolution among the Basoga of Uganda.* Chicago: University of Chicago Press.

FEI, H-T.
  1939 *Peasant Life in China: A Field Study of Country Life in the Yangtze Valley.* New York: E. P. Dutton.

FEI, H-T., AND C. CHANG
  1948 *Earthbound China: A Field Study of Rural Economy in Yunnan.* London: Routledge and Kegan Paul.

FESTINGER, LEON
  1957 *A Theory of Cognitive Dissonance.* Stanford: Stanford University Press.

FOSTER, GEORGE M.
1967 *Tzintzuntzan: Mexican Peasants in a Changing World.* Boston: Little, Brown and Company.

FRANKENBERG, RONALD
1957 *Village on the Border: A Social Study of Religion, Politics, and Football in a North Wales Community.* London: Cohen & West.

FREEDMAN, MAURICE
1967 Immigrants and Associations: Chinese in Nineteenth Century Singapore. In Lloyd Fallers, ed., *Immigrants and Association.* The Hague: Mouton.

FRIEDRICH, PAUL
1965 A Mexican Cacicazgo. *Ethnology* 4:190–209.

GALARZA, ERNESTO
1981 Forecasting Future Cohorts of Mexican Elderly. In Manuel R. Miranda and Ramon A. Ruiz, eds., *Chicano Aging and Mental Health.* Rockville, Md.: U.S. Department of Health and Human Services; Alcohol, Drug Abuse, and Mental Health Administration.

GAMBLE, SIDNEY D.
1944 A Chinese Mutual Savings Society. *Far Eastern Quarterly* 4:41–52.

GEERTZ, CLIFFORD
1962 The Rotating Credit Association: A "Middle Rung" in Development. *Economic Development and Cultural Change* 10:241–263.

GOFFMAN, ERVING
1961 *Asylums: Essays on the Social Situations of Mental Patients and Other Inmates.* Garden City, N.Y.: Doubleday/Anchor.

GOLDSCHMIDT, WALTER F.
1976 The Rural Foundation of American Culture. Gregory Foundation Memorial Lecture, Columbia, Mo.

GONZÁLEZ, NANCIE
1972 Patron–Client Relationships at the International Level. In Arnold Strickon and Sidney M. Greenfield, eds., *Structure and Process in Latin America.* Albuquerque: University of New Mexico Press.

GONZÁLEZ PINEDA, FRANCISCO
1961 *El Mexicano, Psicología de su Destructividad.* Mexico, D.F.: Editorial Pax-Mexico.

GREEN, VERA M.
1969 Aspects of Interethnic Integration in Aruba, Netherlands Antilles. Ph.D. dissertation, University of Arizona.

HAMER, JOHN J.
1967 Voluntary Associations as Structures of Change among the Sidamo of Southwestern Ethiopia. *Anthropological Quarterly* 60: 73–91.

HANDLEMAN, DON
1967 Leadership, Solidarity and Conflict in West Indian Immigrant Associations. *Human Organization* 26:118–125.

HANSEN, ROGER D.
  1971 *The Politics of Mexican Development.* Baltimore: Johns Hopkins
        Press.
HAUSKNECHT, MURRAY
  1962 *The Joiners: A Sociological Description of Voluntary Association Mem-
        bership in the United States.* Totowa, N.J.: Bedminster Press.
HEWES, GORDON W.
  1953– Mexicans in Search of the Mexican. *American Journal of Econom-
  1954   ics and Sociology* 13:209–223.
HOGG, THOMAS CLARK
  1965 Urban Migrants and Associations in Sub-Saharan Africa. Ph.D.
        dissertation, University of Oregon.
HONIGMANN, JOHN J.
  1970 Sampling in Ethnographic Field Work. In R. Naroll and Ronald
        Cohen, eds., *A Handbook of Method in Cultural Anthropology.* New
        York: Columbia University Press.
KAPFERER, BRUCE
  1969 Norms and the Manipulation of Relationships in a Work Con-
        text. In J. Clyde Mitchell, ed., *Social Networks in Urban Situations:
        Analyses of Personal Relationships in Central African Towns.* Man-
        chester: Manchester University Press for the Institute for Social
        Research, University of Zambia.
KATZIN, MARGARET F.
  1959 Partners: An Informal Savings Institution in Jamaica. *Social and
        Economic Studies* 8:436–440.
KENNY, MICHAEL
  1961 Twentieth Century Spanish Expatriates in Cuba: A Sub-cul-
        ture? *Anthropological Quarterly* 34:85–93.
  1962 Twentieth Century Spanish Expatriates in Mexico: An Urban
        Sub-culture. *Anthropological Quarterly* 35:169–180.
KERRI, JAMES N.
  1976 Studying Voluntary Associations as Adaptive Mechanisms: A
        Review of Anthropological Perspectives. *Current Anthropology*
        17:23–47.
KLEIN, LAWRENCE R.
  1947 *The Keynesian Revolution.* New York: Macmillan.
KURTZ, DONALD F.
  1973 The Rotating Credit Association: An Adaptation to Poverty.
        Human Organization 32:49–58.
KURTZ, DONALD F., AND MARGARET SHOWMAN
  1978 The Tanda: A Rotating Credit Association in Mexico. *Ethnology*
        17:65–74.
LEACH, EDMUND R.
  1967 The Language of Kachin Kinship: Reflections on a Tikopia
        Model. In Maurice Freedman, ed., *Social Organization: Essays
        Presented to Raymond Firth.* Chicago: Aldine Publishing Co.

LEEDS, ANTHONY
1965 Brazilian Careers and Social Structure: A Case History and Model. In Dwight B. Heath and Richard N. Adams, eds., *Contemporary Cultures and Societies of Latin America*. New York: Random House.

LEVINE, DONALD N.
1965 *Wax and Gold: Tradition and Innovation in Ethiopian Culture*. Chicago: University of Chicago Press.

LEWIS, OSCAR
1959 *Five Families*. New York: Basic Books.
1961 *Children of Sanchez*. New York: Random House.
1968 *La Vida*. New York: Random House.

LIGHT, IVAN H.
1972 *Ethnic Enterprise in America: Business and Welfare among Chinese, Japanese and Blacks*. Berkeley, Los Angeles, London: University of California Press.

LITTLE, KENNETH
1965 *West African Urbanization: A Study of Voluntary Associations in Social Change*. Cambridge: Cambridge University Press.
1967 *Voluntary Associations in Urban Life: A Case Study in Differential Adaptation*. In Maurice Freedman, ed., *Social Organization: Essays Presented to Raymond Firth*. Chicago: Aldine Publishing Co.
1971 *Some Aspects of African Urbanization South of the Sahara*. Reading, Mass.: Addison-Wesley Modular Publications.

LOMNITZ, LARISSA
1971 Reciprocity of Favors in the Urban Middle Class of Chile. In George Dalton, ed., *Studies in Economic Anthropology*. Anthropological Studies no. 7. Washington, D.C.: American Anthropological Association.
1977 *Networks and Marginality*. Translated by Cinna Lomnitz. New York: Academic Press.

LOMNITZ, LARISSA, AND MARISOL PÉREZ
1974 Historia de una familia de la Ciudad de Mexico. Paper presented at the annual meeting of the American Anthropological Association, Mexico City.

MADSEN, WILLIAM
1962 *The Mexican American of South Texas*. New York: Holt, Rinehart and Winston.

MANGIN, WILLIAM P.
1965 The Role of Regional Associations in the Adaptation of Rural Migrants to Cities in Peru. In Dwight B. Heath and Richard N. Adams, eds., *Contemporary Cultures and Societies of Latin America*. New York: Random House.

MEILLASOUX, CLAUDE
1968 *Urbanization of an African Community: Voluntary Associations in Bamako*. Seattle: University of Washington Press.

MIRACLE, MARVIN P., DIANE S. MIRACLE, AND LAURIE COHEN
1980 Informal Savings Mobilization in Africa. *Economic Development and Cultural Change* 28:701–724.

MITCHELL, J. CLYDE
1969 The Concept and Use of Social Networks. In J. Clyde Mitchell, ed., *Social Networks in Urban Situations: Analyses of Personal Relationships in Central African Towns*. Manchester: Manchester University Press for the Institute for Social Research, University of Zambia.

MOORE, SALLY FAULK
1975 Epilogue: Uncertainties in Situations, Indeterminacies in Culture. In Sally Faulk Moore and Barbara G. Myerhoff, eds., *Symbol and Politics in Communal Ideology, Cases and Questions*. Ithaca and London: Cornell University Press.
1978 *Law as Process*. London: Routledge and Kegan Paul.

MORTON, KEITH L.
1978 Mobilizing Money in a Communal Economy: A Tongan Example. *Human Organization* 37:50–56.

MURPHY, ROBERT
1971 *The Dialectics of Social Life*. New York: Basic Books.

NOBLE, CHARLES
1970 Voluntary Associations of the Basukuma of Northern Mainland Tanzania. Ph.D. dissertation, Catholic University of America.

NORBECK, EDWARD
1966 Rural Japan. In William A. Glaser and David L. Sills, eds., *The Government of Associations: Selections from the Behavioral Sciences*. Totowa, N.J.: Bedminster Press.

ORBACH, MICHAEL K.
1979 Making Extraordinary Decisions in Ordinary Ways: Decision-making as a Natural Process. Unpublished ms.

PARKIN, D. J.
1966 Urban Voluntary Associations as Institutions of Adaptation. *Man*, n.s. 1:91–94.

PAZ, OCTAVIO
1961 *The Labyrinth of Solitude: Life and Thought in Mexico*. New York: Grove Press.

PENNY, D. H.
1968 Farm Credit Policy in the Early Stages of Agricultural Development. *Australian Journal of Agricultural Economics* 12:32–45.

POLANYI, KARL
1957 The Economy as Instituted Process. In Karl Polanyi et al., eds., *Trade and Market in the Early Empires*. Glencoe, Ill.: Free Press.

PRICE-WILLIAMS, DOUGLAS, AND MANUEL RAMIREZ III
1974 Ethnic Differences in Delay of Gratification. *Journal of Social Psychology* 93:23–40.

QUARTERLY ECONOMIC REVIEW OF MEXICO
1979 Annual Supplement: 20.

RAMÍREZ, SANTIAGO
1959 *El Mexicano, Psicología de sus Motivaciones.* Mexico, D. F.: Editorial Pax-Mexico.

LA REVISTA DE MÉRIDA
1900 Caja de Ahorros Monte Piedad de Yucatán Sociedad Coperativa. 9 de Ferbrero: 3.

RUBEL, ARTHUR
1965 *Across the Tracks.* Austin: University of Texas Press.

SAHLINS, MARSHALL
1969 On the Sociology of Primitive Exchange. In Michael Banton, ed., *The Relevance of Models in Social Anthropology.* ASA monograph 1. London: Tavistock.

SAULINIERS, ALFRED H.
1976 *The Economics of Prestation Systems: A Consumer Analysis of Extended Family Obligations with Application to Zaire.* Ann Arbor: Center for Research on Economic Development, University of Michigan.

SCHWARTZ, THEODORE
1968 Beyond Cybernetics: Constructs, Expectations, and Goals in Human Adaptation. Paper prepared for symposium 40, The Effects of Conscious Purpose on Human Adaptation. Wenner-Gren Foundation for Anthropological Research, Burg Wartenstein, Austria.

SKINNER, ELLIOT P.
1974 *African Urban Life: The Transformation of Oaugadougou.* Princeton: Princeton University Press.

SOEN, DAN, AND PATRICE DE CAMARAMOND
1972 Savings Associations among the Bamileke: Traditional and Modern Cooperations in the Southwest Cameroon. *American Anthropologist* 74:1170–1179.

TREUDLEY, MARY
1966 The Transformation of Peasants into Citizens. In William A. Glaser and David L. Sills, eds., *The Government of Associations: Selections from the Behavioral Sciences.* Totowa, N.J.: Bedminster Press.

U.S., DEPARTMENT OF COMMERCE, BUREAU OF THE CENSUS
1979 *Persons of Spanish Origin in the United States: March 1978. Population Characteristics.* Washington, D.C.: U.S. Government Printing Office.

VÉLEZ-IBAÑEZ, CARLOS G.
1978a Amigos Politicos o Amigos Sociales: The Politics of Putting Someone in Your Pocket—Strategies of Power among Brokers in Central Urbanizing Mexico. *Human Organization* 37:268–277.

1978b Youth and Aging in Central Mexico: One Day in the Life of Four Families of Migrants. In Barbara Myerhoff and André Simic, eds., *Life's Career—Aging: Cultural Variations on Growing Old.* Beverly Hills and London: Sage Publications.

1980 Mexican/Hispano Support Systems and Confianza: Theoretical Issues of Cultural Adaptation. In Ramon Valle and William Vega, eds., *Hispanic Natural Support Systems: Mental Health Promotion Perspectives.* Sacramento: California Department of Mental Health.

1982 Social Diversity, Commercialization, and Organizational Complexity of Urban Mexican/Chicano Rotating Credit Associations: Theoretical and Empirical Issues of Adaptation. *Human Organization* 41:107–120.

1983 *Rituals of Marginality: Politics, Process and Culture Change in Central Urban Mexico.* Berkeley: University of California Press.

VÉLEZ-IBAÑEZ, CARLOS G., RICHARD VERDUGO, AND FRANCISCO NUÑEZ

1981 Politics and Mental Health among Elderly Chicanos. In Manual R. Miranda and Ramon N. Ruiz, eds., *Chicano Aging and Mental Health.* Rockville, Md.: U.S. Department of Health and Human Services; Alcohol, Drug Abuse, and Mental Health Administration.

WALLACE, ANTHONY F. C.

1961 *Culture and Personality.* New York: Random House.

WALLERSTEIN, EMANUEL M.

1966 Voluntary Associations. In James S. Coleman and Carl G. Rosenberg, Jr., eds., *Political Parties and National Integration in Tropical Africa.* Berkeley: University of California Press.

WEAVER, THOMAS, AND THEODORE DOWNING

1977 *Mexican Migration.* Tucson: Bureau of Ethnic Research, Department of Anthropology, University of Arizona.

WHEELDON, P. D.

1969 The Operation of Voluntary Associations and Personal Networks in the Political Processes of an Inter-Ethnic Community. In J. Clyde Mitchell, ed., *Social Networks in Urban Situations: Analyses of Personal Relationships in Central African Towns.* Manchester: Manchester University Press for the Institute for Social Research, University of Zambia.

WOLF, ERIC R.

1956 Aspects of Group Relations in a Complex Society: Mexico. *American Anthropologist* 58:1065–1078.

1959 *Sons of the Shaking Earth.* Chicago: University of Chicago Press.

WU, DAVID Y. H.

1974 To Kill Three Birds with One Stone: The Rotating Credit Associations of the Papua New Guinea Chinese. *American Ethnologist* 1:565–584.

Index